Time & Money *Sanders*

Grades 1-2

By
Bill Linderman

Cover Illustration by
Laura Zarrin

Published by Instructional Fair • TS Denison
an imprint of

 Children's Publishing

Author: Bill Linderman
Editors: Kathryn Wheeler, Meredith Van Zomeren, Wendy Roh Jenks
Cover Illustration: Laura Zarrin
Inside Illustrations: Tim Foley

 Children's Publishing

Published by Instructional Fair • TS Denison
An imprint of McGraw-Hill Children's Publishing
Copyright © 2000 McGraw-Hill Children's Publishing

Send all inquiries to:
McGraw-Hill Children's Publishing
3195 Wilson Drive NW
Grand Rapids, Michigan 49544

Time & Money—grades 1–2
ISBN: 1-56822-904-6

4 5 6 7 8 9 10 PHXBK 09 08 07 06 05 04

Table of Contents

Time

Time Flies (comparing time memories) 4–5
Time for Tasks! (comparing less time to more) 6–7
Meet a Minute! (minutes) 8–9
What Machine Measures Time? (clock) 10
Two Hands to Tell Time (clock hands) 11
Hour Power (hours) 12–13
On the Hour (elapsed time in hours) 14–15
Mystery of the Missing Hands (clock hands) 16–17
Half the Story! (half-hours) 18–19
Half-Hour Stories (elapsed time in half-hours) 20–21
Tortoise and Hare Race! (half-hour increments) 22–23
A Half-Hour = 30 Minutes! (half-hours) 24–25
Half of a Half! (quarter-hours) 26–27
Quarter-Hour Hero (elapsed time in quarter-
hours) 28–29
Give Me "Five! (five-minute increments) 30–31
Halfway Around the Clock (five-minute increments
to thirty minutes) 32–33
What a Time With Chiggles (recognizing times) 34–35
What a Mess! (sequencing time intervals) 36–37
All Kinds of Clocks (digital clocks) 38–39
Reading Time (relating dial and digital times) ... 40–41
What's the Time? (telling time to the hour) 42–43
Let's Play with Days! (days of the week) 44–45
Working with Weeks (one week) 46–47
My Favorite Month (months) 48
Calendar Clues (relating months to events) 49
Now You Know Time! (time: review) 50–51

Money

One Wonderful Penny (penny) 52–53
Pennies Add Up! (adding pennies by 1s) 54
More Pennies to Add (adding pennies by 1s) 55
Next Up—Nickels! (nickel) 56–57
Toy Trade (adding nickels by 5s) 58–59
Making Cents (writing cent signs) 60–61
Want to Munch Some Lunch? (value of pennies
and nickels) 62–63
Dimes on Deck (dime) 64–65
A Dime at a Time (adding dimes by 10s) 66–67
Birthday Buying (value of coins) 68–69
Can It Be Done? (adding coin values) 70–71
Pennies, Nickels, and Dimes (coins: review) 72
Coin Stories (recognizing coins and values) 73
Let's Count! (adding coin values) 74–75
Mystery Coins! (adding and subtracting values)76–77
Meet the Quarter! (quarter) 78–79
Big Pig Banking! (adding quarters with other
coins) 80–81
Money Mom (adding coins to 25¢) 82–83
Quarters Have Cent Power (comparing values) 84–85
All Quarters Are Worth the Same (introduction of
changing coin designs) 86–87
Zooming Down Cents Lane! (adding cent values) 88
Cents-ible Racing (adding cent values) 89
Cents at the Park! (subtracting cent values) 90–91
Spending Money Is Subtracting (spending) 92–93
A Store Story (adding and subtracting money) 94–95
A Diller, a Dollar! (dollar) 96–97
Birthday Surprise (adding dollar values) 98–99
What Is Money? (concept of money) 100–101
Money on Parade! (money: review) 102–103
Answer Key 104–128

Name _____

Time Flies

Time moves even when we are asleep. It always moves at the same rate. On some days, time seems to go slowly, but on other days, time flies!

Color the picture from each pair that shows time when it feels fast.

Name _____

Color the picture from each pair that shows time when it feels fast.

Name _____

Time for Tasks!

Do you help at home? Some chores take more time than others.

Color the picture from each pair that shows the job that would take less time to do.

Name _____

Color the picture from each pair that shows the job that would take less time to do.

7

Name _____

Meet a Minute!

Have you ever heard someone say, "Just a minute"? What does that mean?

How long is a minute? Let's find out!

Ask an adult to time you. Then count the number of times you do each thing for a whole minute. Write the answer on the line.

I hopped _____ times in one minute.

I tapped my shoulder _____ times in one minute.

Name _____

Write your answers
on the lines.

I touched my toes _____
times in one minute.

I picked up _____ sticks in
one minute.

I put away _____ toys in
one minute.

What Machine Measures Time?

Use these words with the clock to fill in the blanks:

circle	**hands**	**12**
face	**6**	**clock**

This machine works all day and all night.
We never turn it off.

It has a _____ (A),
but no eyes and no nose!

It has _____ (B, C), but no fingers.

The little hand (B) is pointing to _____ .

The big hand (C) is pointing to _____ .

This machine is shaped like a _____ . (D)

This machine is called a _____ .

Name _____

Two Hands to Tell Time

A clock needs two hands to tell us the time.

The big hand is called the minute hand.
Find the minute hand and color it **purple**.

The little hand is called the hour hand.
Find the hour hand and color it **yellow**.

On this clock, the minute hand is pointing to the number _____ .

The hour hand is pointing to the number _____ .

That's how a clock tells us it is 9 o'clock.

On this clock, the minute hand is pointing to the number _____ .

The hour hand is pointing to the number _____ .

That's how a clock tells us it is 3 o'clock.

Name _____

Hour Power

When the minute hand points to 12, it's the start of a brand new hour! The hour hand points to the name of the hour.

Look at the clock.

Circle the hour: **6   7**

The minute hand is on _____ . The hour hand is on _____.

It is _____o'clock.

Now look at these clocks:

It is _____o'clock.

It is _____o'clock.

Name _____

Hour Power cont.

Circle the correct hour on each clock.

1   **2**

3   **4**

5   **6**

7   **8**

9   **10**

11   **12**

Name _____

On the Hour

Draw the hour hand on each clock.

The hour hand is on 2.

The hour hand is on 4.

The hour hand is on 6.

The hour hand is on 7.

The hour hand is on 9.

The hour hand is on 11.

Name _____

What do clocks do best?

Find out! Write down each time. Fill in the blanks at the bottom with the letter that matches each time.

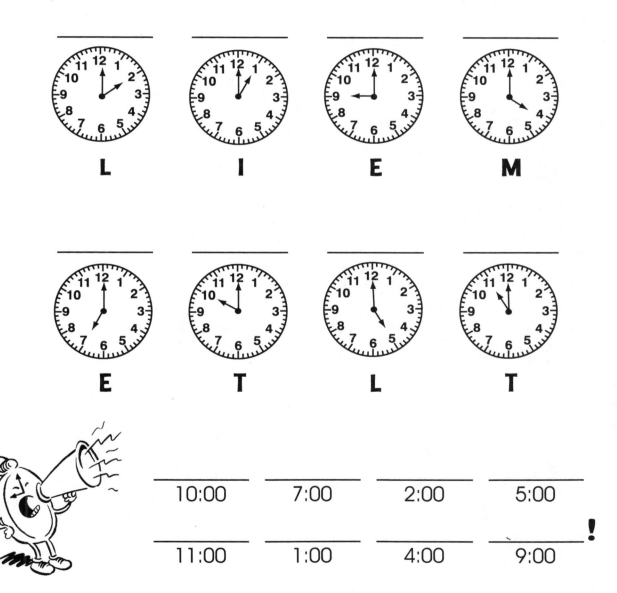

_____   _____   _____   _____

L   I   E   M

_____   _____   _____   _____

E   T   L   T

_____	_____	_____	_____
10:00	7:00	2:00	5:00

_____	_____	_____	_____ !
11:00	1:00	4:00	9:00

Mystery of the Missing Hands

Oh, no! Someone took half the clock hands!

 You can help. Draw the missing hand for each clock.

It is 1 o'clock.

It is 6 o'clock.

It is 2 o'clock.

It is 9 o'clock.

Name _____

Clue: When both the minute and the hour hand are pointing to 12, it is 12:00.

It is 3 o'clock.

It is 10 o'clock.

It is 5 o'clock.

It is 7 o'clock.

It is 8 o'clock.

It is 12 o'clock.

Name _____

Half the Story!

When the minute hand moves all the way around the clock face, that's one hour. When it moves only halfway, that's called a half-hour.

This clock face shows that a half-hour has passed since 8 o'clock. See how the hour hand moves too?

What number is the minute hand on? _____

We have different ways of saying the time at the half-hour.

- Sometimes we say, "It is half past 8."

- Sometimes we say, "It is 8 thirty."

- A half-hour is written like this: 8:30.

  That means 30 minutes have gone by since 8 o'clock.

What time does this clock show?

Half past _____ .

Name _____

What time is it?

It is half past _____ .

It is _____ :30.

It is half past _____ .

It is _____ :30.

If your bedtime is 8:30, where would the hands be on this clock when it's time for bed?
Draw them:

Name _____

Half-Hour Stories

Can you keep track of the time in these stories?

Mark started a sand castle at 12 o'clock.

Write the time: _____ :00

At half past 12, Mark's mother said, "Lunch time!"

Write the time: _____ :30

Mark put a flag on his castle at 1 o'clock.

Write the time: _____ :00

Half-Hour Stories cont.

Name _____

Draw the clock hands to show times in this story.

Maria and Chung walked to the park at 2 o'clock.

The time is 2:00.

They played on the swings until half past 2.

The time is 2:30.

Chung played on the slide at 3 o'clock.

The time is 3:00.

Maria said, "Let's race home!" They got home at half past 3.

The time is 3:30.

Name _____

Tortoise and Hare Race!

They are at the starting line! Can you write the times to show each part of the race?

They are off!

Hare runs up the hill.

Tortoise plods along.

Hare falls asleep.

Tortoise crosses the finish line!

Hare wakes up. "Oh, no!"

Name _____

Why do rabbits eat carrot greens?

Fill in each blank with the letter that matches the correct time.

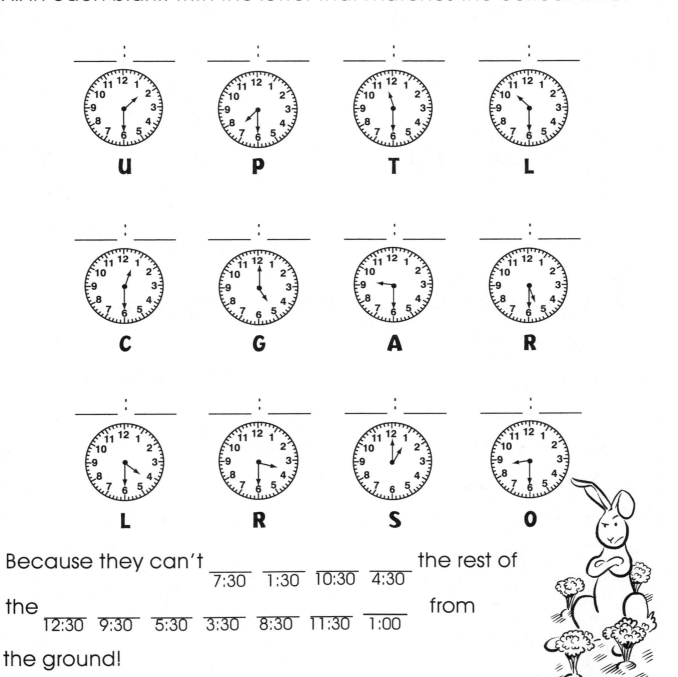

Because they can't ____ ____ ____ ____ the rest of
               7:30 1:30 10:30 4:30

the ____ ____ ____ ____ ____ ____ ____ from
   12:30 9:30 5:30 3:30 8:30 11:30 1:00

the ground!

Name _____

A Half-Hour = 30 Minutes

Eva practices piano at: ____ : ____	Pam eats lunch at: ____ : ____
David does his homework at: ____ : ____	Earl reads each night at: ____ : ____

1. What time does David start his homework?
   _____ o'clock

2. If David works for thirty minutes, what time does he finish?
   _____

3. If Eva plays piano for thirty minutes each day, what time does she stop? _____

4. If Pam has thirty minutes for lunch, what time is lunch over? _____

5. If Earl reads for a half-hour each night, what time does he finish? _____

A Half-Hour = 30 Minutes cont.

Name _____

Sam eats lunch at 12:00. Thirty minutes later, he is back in class. What time does lunch end?

____ : ____

It took Alexa thirty minutes to set up her dolls. She was done at 2:30. What time did she start?

____ : ____

David made a sand castle. He worked for thirty minutes. He finished at 11:00. What time did he start?

____ : ____

Martha and her mother bake bread. The bread bakes for thirty minutes. If they put the bread in the oven at 3:30, what time will it be done?

____ : ____

Name _____

Half of a Half!

There are two half-hours in one hour.

Color one
half-hour
red.

Color the
other
half-hour
blue.

How many quarter-hours are in one hour?

Let's find out!

Color one quarter-hour **yellow**.

Color one quarter-hour **green**.

Color one quarter-hour **orange**.

Color one quarter-hour **purple**.

How many quarter-hours did you color?

1   2   3   4

Now draw lines to
divide this clock into
quarter-hours!

Half of a Half! cont.

Name _____

Each quarter-hour is 15 minutes. From the 12 to the 3 on a clock is the first quarter-hour.

5 minutes
10 minutes
15 minutes

We say, "It is quarter past 9."

We write it like this: 9:15.

Draw the hands.

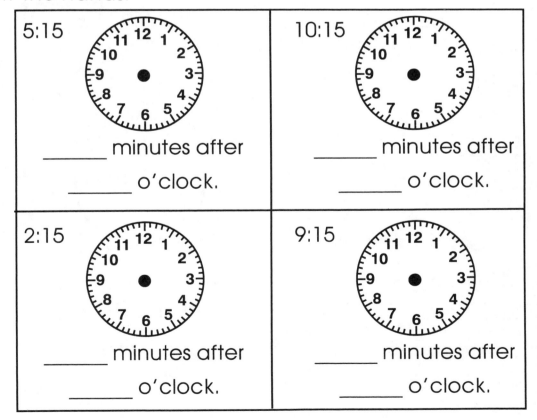

5:15

_____ minutes after

_____ o'clock.

10:15

_____ minutes after

_____ o'clock.

2:15

_____ minutes after

_____ o'clock.

9:15

_____ minutes after

_____ o'clock.

Name _____

Quarter-Hour Hero

Follow Wonder Worm through a day!

Wonder Worm fixes
a bridge!

The time is ____ :15.

Wonder Worm saves
a planet!

The time is ____ :15.

Wonder Worm stops
a flood!

The time is ____ :15.

Wonder Worm takes
time for lunch!

The time is ____ :15.

Quarter-Hour Hero cont.

Name _____

Wonder Worm finds
a lost kitten!

The time is ____ :15.

Wonder Worm puts out
a fire!

The time is ____ :15.

Wonder Worm is on the
news!

The time is ____ :15.

Wonder Worm needs
his sleep!

The time is ____ :15.

Draw the hands on the clock:

Wonder Worm's
lunch time: _____

Wonder Worm's
bedtime: _____

Name _____

Give Me "Five"!

Do you remember how many minutes are in a half-hour? You can always find out by counting each five-minute space between the clock numbers. Count by 5s to fill in the boxes.

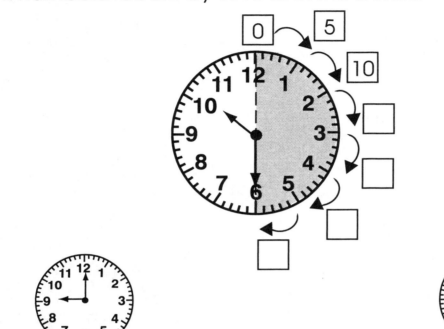

Tell the time:

_____ : _____

Five minutes later:

_____ : **0 5**

Start from 12, and count by 5s to see how many minutes past the hour the minute hand has moved.

____ : ____   ____ : ____   ____ : ____

Give Me "Five"! cont.

Name _____

What's the first thing you should do in the morning when you wake up?

To solve the puzzle, write down each time. Then, fill in the blanks with the letters that match the times. Use the pictures and letters to say the answer out loud!

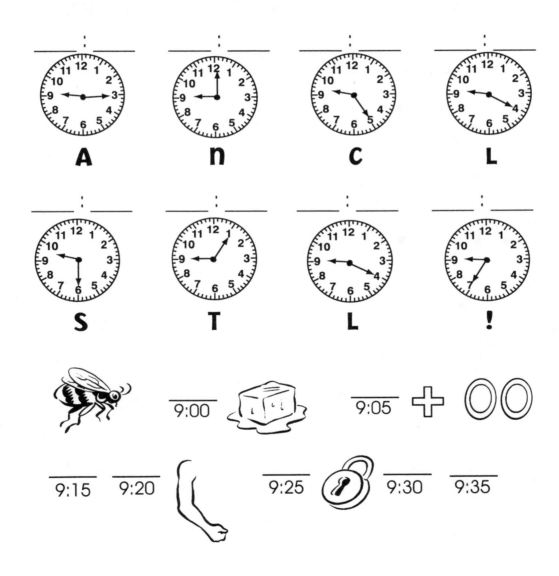

A **n** **c** **L**

S **T** **L** **!**

9:00   9:05 ➕ 00

9:15   9:20   9:25   9:30   9:35

Name _____

Halfway Around the Clock

There are five minutes between each number on the face of a clock... so count by 5s to count halfway around!

5 minutes
10 minutes
15 minutes
20 minutes
25 minutes
30 minutes

When you count halfway around the clock, that's a half-hour!

A half-hour is _____ minutes.

What time does this clock say? ____ : ____

Now show the time 30 minutes later. Draw the hands.

Halfway Around the Clock cont.   Name _____

Travel the paths. Match each clock with the time a half-hour later.

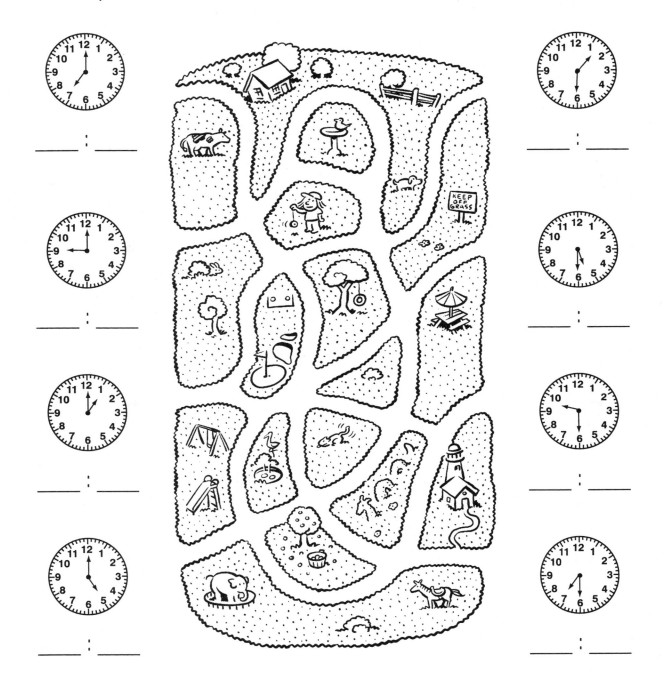

_____ : _____

_____ : _____

_____ : _____

_____ : _____

_____ : _____

_____ : _____

_____ : _____

_____ : _____

Name _____

What a Time with Chiggles

Fill in the blanks with the correct times. Then write the letter for each time in the correct space on page 35, in the story about David's new puppy, Chiggles.

___ : ___

U

___ : ___

T

___ : ___

A

___ : ___

E

___ : ___

O

___ : ___

C

___ : ___

D

___ : ___

G

Name _____

What a day! Dad came home with Chiggles, our new puppy, at 8:05 _____. She has a big wet nose and floppy ears. Dad said at 8:10 _____ that I could take her for a walk.

At 8:15, _____ the phone rang. It was Alesha. She wanted to meet Chiggles right away.

Alesha came over at 8:30 _____. I showed her my new friend!

Alesha and I played with Chiggles. Then we saw that it was 8:55 _____. Five minutes later, we took our walk to the park on that sunny, warm day.

By 9:10 _____, Chiggles was chasing butterflies and squirrels. Lots of people stopped to pet Chiggles. We got home at 9:35 _____ .

Alesha went home. Then I sat on the porch swing, holding my puppy. Chiggles fell asleep with her nose against my neck. The clock said 10:20 _____ . That's the last thing I remember, because I fell asleep, too!

Write the letters from the blanks on page 34 in order to see what Chiggles will be when she grows up:

___ ___ ___ ___ ___ ___ ___ ___!

Name _____

What a Mess!

Help clean up the clock room. Write down each time. Then number the row of clocks from 1 to 3, with 1 as the earliest time. Write **1, 2,** or **3** in each box.

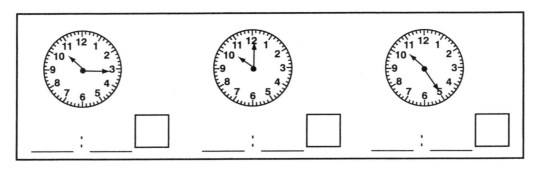

_____ : _____   ☐   _____ : _____   ☐   _____ : _____   ☐

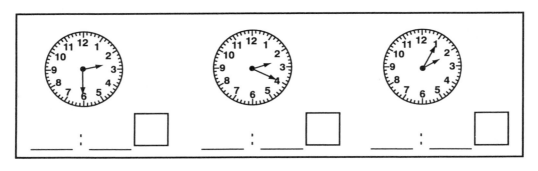

_____ : _____   ☐   _____ : _____   ☐   _____ : _____   ☐

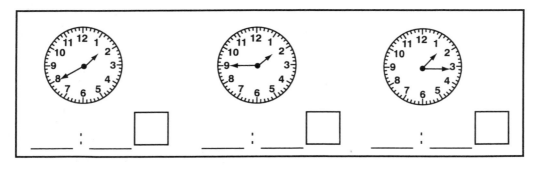

_____ : _____   ☐   _____ : _____   ☐   _____ : _____   ☐

Name _____

Write each time. Then write **1**, **2**, or **3** in each box, with 1 being the earliest time.

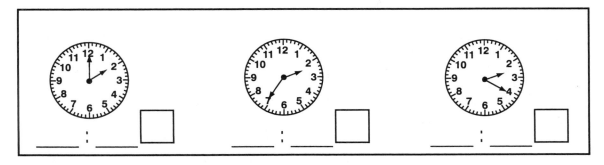

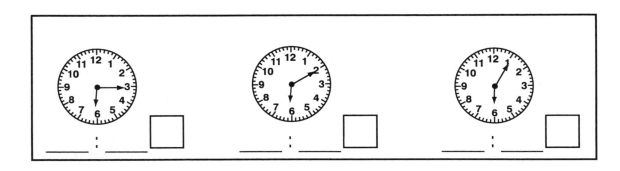

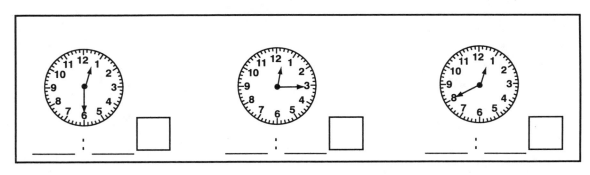

Name _____

All Kinds of Clocks

Clocks tell us the time,
No matter how it flies.
A clock will show the time for bed,
And when the sun will rise.

Clocks tell the time for breakfast,
And lunch and dinner too.
What times of day, of work and play,
Are these clocks telling you?

There are all kinds of clocks. Circle the ones you have seen.

Name _____

Dial clocks look like this:

Digital clocks look like this:

If you have a watch, is it dial or digital?
Circle the correct picture:

Tell the time on each digital clock below:

_____ o'clock

_____ o'clock

_____ o'clock

_____ o'clock

Name _____

Reading Time

On a dial clock, you look at the hands to read the time.

It is _____ o'clock.

On a digital clock, the numbers say the time.

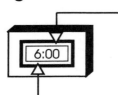

These are the minutes. When they are both zero, you say "o'clock."

This is the hour.

When a digital clock shows quarter-hours and half-hours, it shows them as minutes.

A quarter-hour is _____ minutes. This is the same time as "It is a quarter past _____ ."

A half-hour is _____ minutes.

This is the time, "It is half past _____ ."

Write the times in the digital faces.

1.

"It is half past two."

2.

"It is quarter past eleven."

3.

"It is 3 o'clock."

Reading Time cont.

Name _____

Draw a line to each matching time.

2:15

3:00

11:00

8:15

9:30

Name _____

What's the Time?

Mark eats breakfast at ____ : ____ .

What time do you eat breakfast? ____ : ____ .

Pedro goes to school at ____ : ____ .

What time do you leave for school? ____ : ____ .

Pam's lunch recess starts at ____ : ____ .

What time does your lunch recess start? ____ : ____ .

Sue's school day ends at ____ : ____ .

What time does your school day end? ____ : ____ .

Name _____

Circle the clock that best answers each question.

1. Monica wakes up each morning at this time.

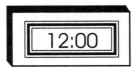   12:00   2:00   7:00

2. Sarah walks her puppy right after school at this time.

   11:00   8:00   3:00

3. David goes to bed each night at this time.

   8:00   12:00   1:00

4. Lee's family sits down to eat dinner at this time.

   6:00   9:00   3:00

5. Eva plays the piano each afternoon at this time.

   4:00   8:00   9:00

Name _____

Let's Play with Days!

How long is a day? One day is 24 hours long!

You can do many things in one day.

Can you do all these things in one day?
Circle **yes** or **no** at the bottom of the page.

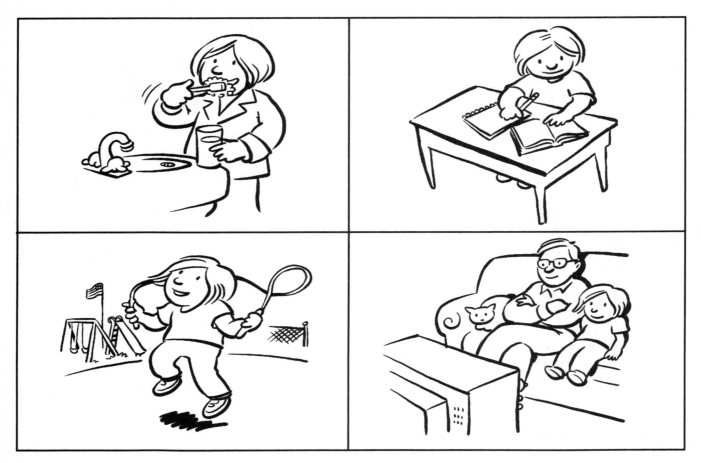

Yes   no

Now color the pictures!

You have a name. So does each day.

Ask an adult to read you the names of the days. Then look at the pictures. Draw a line from each picture to the day when that might happen.

Sunday	Monday	Tuesday	Wednesday	Thursday	Friday	Saturday
1	2	3	4	5	6	7

What is your favorite day? Color its square in your favorite color!

Write its name here.

_____

_____

Name _____

Working with Weeks

Here is one week on a calendar. Count the days:

Sunday	Monday	Tuesday	Wednesday	Thursday	Friday	Saturday
1	2	3	4	5	6	7

How many days are there in one week?   1   3   5   7

Here are the days of the week. Write the number of each day in the blank to show its correct order. Start with Sunday as 1.

Monday _____

Saturday _____

Thursday _____

Tuesday _____

Sunday _____

Friday _____

Wednesday _____

Working with Weeks cont.

Name _____

Let's rocket through a week! Work through the maze by going from one day of the week to the next, in order.

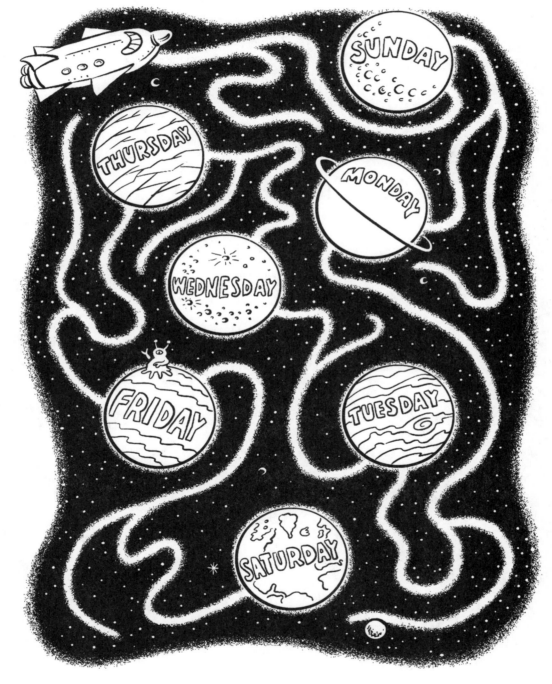

Name _____

My Favorite Month

Days and weeks turn into **months**. Most months have 30 or 31 days. Here are all the months in one year! Count them.

How many months in a year? _____ Now number the months in order, starting with January as **1**.

January

April

February

March

May

June

July

August

October

September

November

December

Name _____

Calendar Clues

A calendar counts days and months, just like a clock counts minutes and hours.

Here are the months on a calendar:

January	February	March	April
	BE MINE		
May	**June**	**July**	**August**
September	**October**	**November**	**December**

What month does school start ? Color that month **yellow**!

In what month is Valentine's Day ? Color that month **pink**!

In what month is Halloween ? Color that month **orange**!

In what month is Thanksgiving ? Color that month **red**!

Name _____

Now You Know Time!

hour

half-hour

quarter-hour

Circle the correct numbers.

How many minutes in an hour?   **15   30   60**

How many minutes in a half-hour?   **15   30   60**

How many minutes in a quarter-hour? **15   30   60**

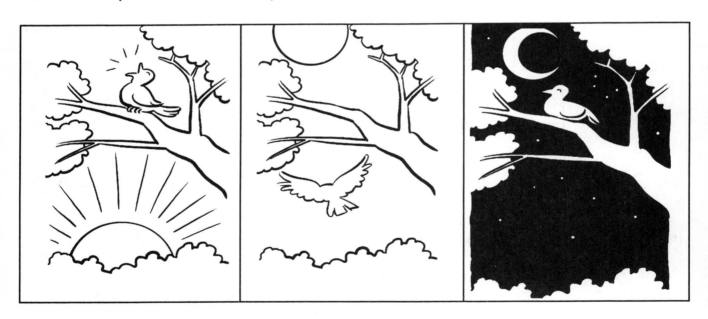

How many hours in a day?   **6   12   24   48**

Now You Know Time ! cont.

Name _____

Sunday 1	Monday 2	Tuesday 3	Wednesday 4	Thursday 5	Friday 6	Saturday 7

What day comes after Monday? _____

What day comes before Friday? _____

What day comes between Tuesday and Thursday? _____

How many days in a week? **2   4   6   7   8   9**

January

February
BE MINE

March

April

May

June

July

August

September

October

November

December

What month comes before May? _____

What month comes after December? _____

How many months in a year?   **3   6   8   12**

Name _____

One Wonderful Penny

Yes, I'm a penny!
Count me by ones,
And when you are done,
You can spend me,
Or lend me,
Or buy bubblegum!

This is a **penny**.

Ask for a real penny, and lay it on the pictures.
Look at both sides of the penny.

A penny is worth 1 cent, so we count pennies by ones.

Count the pennies. Then write how many on the line.

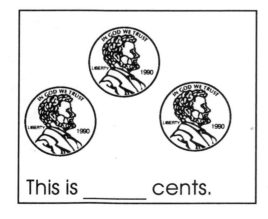

This is _____ cents.

This is _____ cents.

One Wonderful Penny cont.

Name _____

Circle the correct amount of pennies.

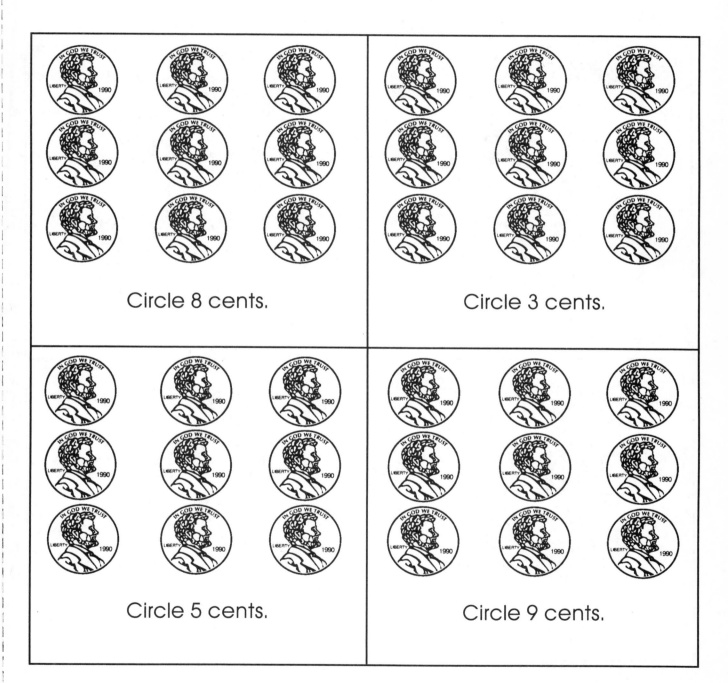

Circle 8 cents.

Circle 3 cents.

Circle 5 cents.

Circle 9 cents.

Name _____

Pennies Add Up!

Find the pennies in each picture. Add them up.

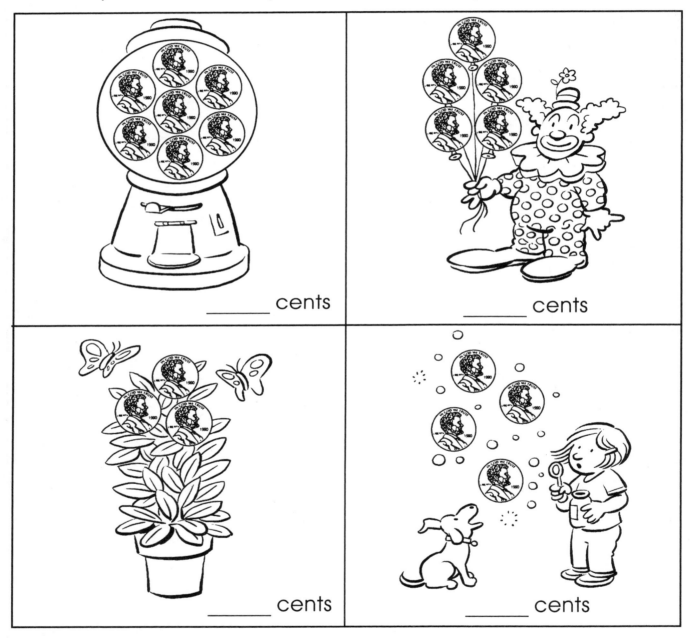

_____ cents

_____ cents

_____ cents

_____ cents

Now color the pictures!

Name _____

More Pennies to Add!

Add the pennies in each picture.

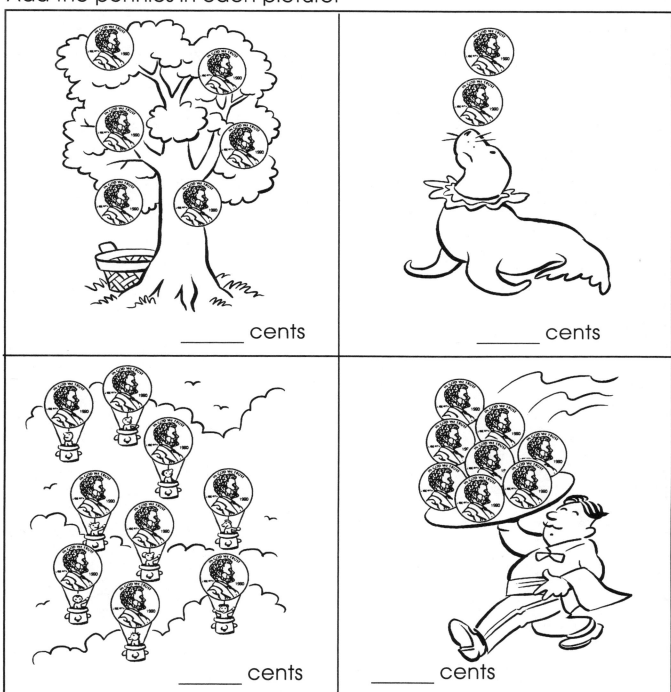

_____ cents

_____ cents

_____ cents

_____ cents

Now color the pictures!

55   IF87110 *Time & Money*

Name _____

Next Up—Nickels!

This is a **nickel**.

Ask for a real nickel, and lay it on the pictures.
Look at both sides of the nickel.

A nickel is worth 5 cents, so we count nickels by fives. Count the nickels like this: **5   10   15   20**

Then write how much they are worth on the line.

This is _____ cents.

This is _____ cents.

This is _____ cents.

This is _____ cents.

Name _____

Circle the correct amount of the nickels.

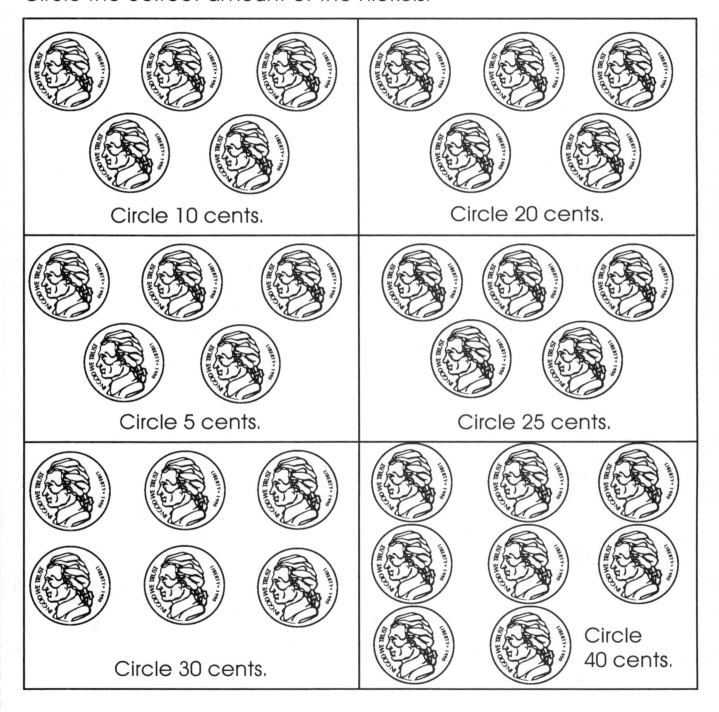

Circle 10 cents.

Circle 20 cents.

Circle 5 cents.

Circle 25 cents.

Circle 30 cents.

Circle 40 cents.

Name _____

Toy Trade

Let's take nickels to the school toy trade!

Count the nickels. How many do you have?

You have _____ nickels. That's 50 cents!

Put **X**s through the nickels you spend for each toy.

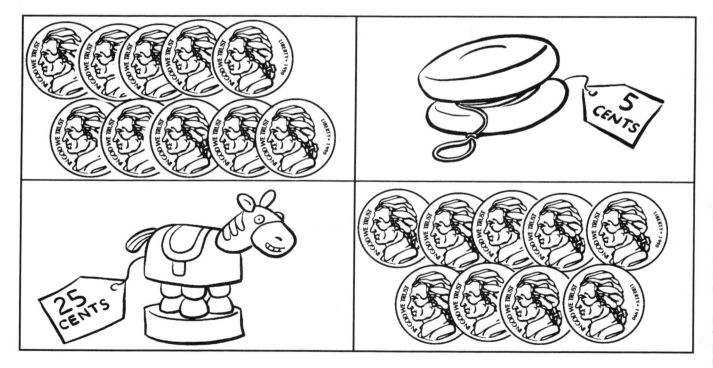

Toy Trade cont.

Name _____

Put Xs through the nickels you spend.

Uh, oh! Did you run out of nickels?

To buy the robot, how many more nickels do you need? Circle them.

Name _____

Making Cents

One penny is 1 cent. We write 1 cent like this: **1¢**

Color all the shapes with pennies and nickels **blue**.

Color all the other shapes **red**.

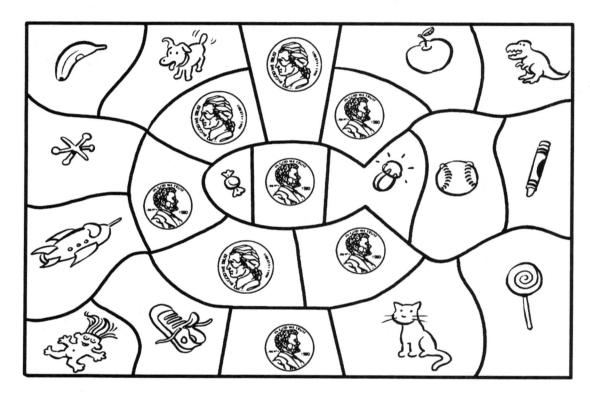

Did you find the cent sign? Now practice writing **¢**.

One penny is   1 _____.

Two pennies is 2 _____.

One nickel is   5 _____.

Name _____

Look at each group of money. Write the amount in cents. The first one is done for you.

This is __**4¢**__.

This is _____.

This is _____.

This is _____.

This is _____.

Name _____

Want to Munch Some Lunch?

Lunch money jingles when
you walk down the hall.
Its bright, ringing sound is
a time-for-lunch call.
What will you buy?
What will you munch?
It depends on the money you
have to buy lunch!

Circle each food choice after you count your money.

Pick something to drink!

You have:

That's

_____ ¢.

 20¢ 15¢ 25¢

Pick your main course!

You have:

That's

_____ ¢.

 40¢  30¢  35¢

Want to Munch Some Lunch? cont.

Name _____

Circle each food choice after you count your money.

Pick a fruit or vegetable!

You have:

That's

_____ ¢.

 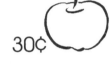 

25¢   30¢   35¢

Pick a dessert!

You have:

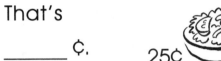

That's

_____ ¢.

25¢   10¢   20¢

Hey! You find this coin in your pocket.

What can you buy with it?
Circle the treat
you can buy.

20¢   5¢   15¢

Name _____

Dimes on Deck

This is a **dime**. Ask for a real dime, and lay it on the pictures. Look at both sides of the dime.

A dime is worth 10 cents, so we count dimes by tens. Like this:

10   20   30   40

Count the dimes in each box. Then write the total on each line.

This is _____ cents.

This is _____ cents.

This is _____ cents.

This is _____ cents.

Name _____

Circle the correct number of dimes.

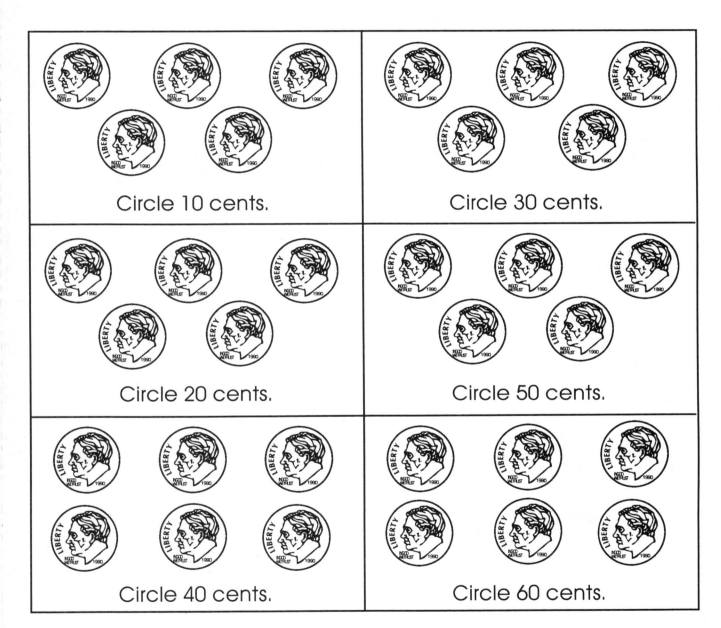

Circle 10 cents.

Circle 30 cents.

Circle 20 cents.

Circle 50 cents.

Circle 40 cents.

Circle 60 cents.

Name _____

A Dime at a Time

Count the dimes. Write the amount in cents. The first one is done for you.

This is **20¢** .	This is _____ .	This is _____ .
This is _____ .	This is _____ .	This is _____ .

A Dime at a Time cont.

Name _____

Count the dimes in each box. Write the totals in cents.

This is _____ .   This is _____ .   This is _____ .

Molly wants to buy a Mother's Day card for 50¢.
Circle the dimes she will need.

Shane wants to buy a comic book. It costs 80¢.
Circle the dimes he will need.

Kendra wants to save 40¢ to put in her bank.
Circle the dimes she will need.

Name _____

Birthday Buying

Alexa, Sam, and Mark are all going to Kim's birthday party. Help them buy presents. Draw **X**s through the money they need to buy each gift.

1.

2.

3.

Birthday Buying cont.

Name _____

Draw **X**s through the money needed to buy each gift.

4.

5.

6.

7.

Name _____

Can It Be Done?

Mrs. Fox's students want to buy her a baby gift. Each student needs to bring in 35 cents. Draw **X**s through each student's coins to equal 35 cents.

1.   Here is Maria's money.

2.   Here is Chung's money.

3.   Here is Alexa's money.

Name _____

Draw **X**s through each student's coins to equal 35 cents.

4. Here is Kim's money.

5. Here is Sam's money.

6. Here is Kendra's money.

Hint: The quarter is worth 25 pennies!

7. Does every student have 35 cents?   **Yes**   **No**

8. Who has the most money? _____

9. Who has the least money?_____

Name _____

Pennies, Nickels, and Dimes

Here are the fronts and backs of three coins.

Circle the value for each coin.

Penny	1¢	5¢	10¢
Nickel	1¢	5¢	10¢
Dime	1¢	5¢	10¢

Circle each group of coins that has a value of 5¢.

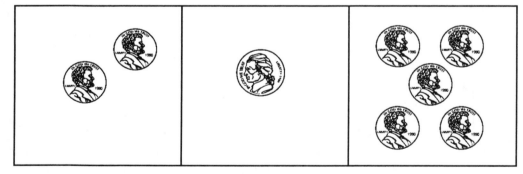

Circle each group of coins that has a value of 10¢.

Name _____

Coin Stories

Circle the answer for each story.

1. Lee loves to draw pictures of kittens.
   Her friend Maria gives her one cent for each kitten picture.
   Circle the coin that Lee gets for one picture.

2. Mark puts all his nickels in a special piggy bank.
   Circle this coin.

3. Chung has the smallest of all U.S. coins. It is worth ten cents. She
   could trade it for two nickels or ten pennies.
   Circle this coin.

4. David wants to buy a peppermint candy. It is 15 cents.
   Circle the two coins he will have to spend.

Color the correct number of coins to equal each value below.

Nickel =

Dime =

Name _____

Let's Count!

Add the coins together. Count by 1s, 5s, or 10s.

1. = _____ ¢

2. = _____ ¢

3. = _____ ¢

4. = _____ ¢

5. = _____ ¢

6. = _____ ¢

IF87110 *Time & Money*

Name _____

As you add each coin, write down the new total.

Example:

10   20   25   30   35   = _____ ¢

1.

_____ _____ _____ _____ _____   = _____ ¢

2.

_____ _____ _____ _____ _____   = _____ ¢

3.

_____ _____ _____ _____ _____   = _____ ¢

4.

_____ _____ _____ _____ _____   = _____ ¢

5.

_____ _____ _____ _____ _____   = _____ ¢

Name _____

Mystery Coins

Find each mystery coin. Count the coins shown. Subtract that amount from the total shown.

1. = 36¢

    36¢

    − [ ]

    Mystery coin value: _____ ¢

2. = 20¢

    20¢

    − [ ]

    Mystery coin value: _____ ¢

3. = 45¢

    45¢

    − [ ]

    Mystery coin value: _____ ¢

4. = 28¢

    28¢

    − [ ]

    Mystery coin value: _____ ¢

5. = 60¢

    60¢

    − [ ]

    Mystery coin value: _____ ¢

Name _____

Subtract the value of the coins from the total to find the mystery coin.

6. = 40¢

$$\begin{array}{r} 40¢ \\ - \quad\quad \\ \hline \end{array}$$

Mystery coin value: _____ ¢

7. = 25¢

$$\begin{array}{r} 25¢ \\ - \quad\quad \\ \hline \end{array}$$

Mystery coin value: _____ ¢

8. = 37¢

$$\begin{array}{r} 37¢ \\ - \quad\quad \\ \hline \end{array}$$

Mystery coin value: _____ ¢

9. = 55¢

$$\begin{array}{r} 55¢ \\ - \quad\quad \\ \hline \end{array}$$

Mystery coin value: _____ ¢

10. = 40¢

$$\begin{array}{r} 40¢ \\ - \quad\quad \\ \hline \end{array}$$

Mystery coin value: _____ ¢

Name _____

Dive into Quarters!

This is a quarter. Ask for a real quarter, and lay it on the pictures. Look at both sides of the quarter.

A quarter is worth 25¢. That's a lot for one coin!

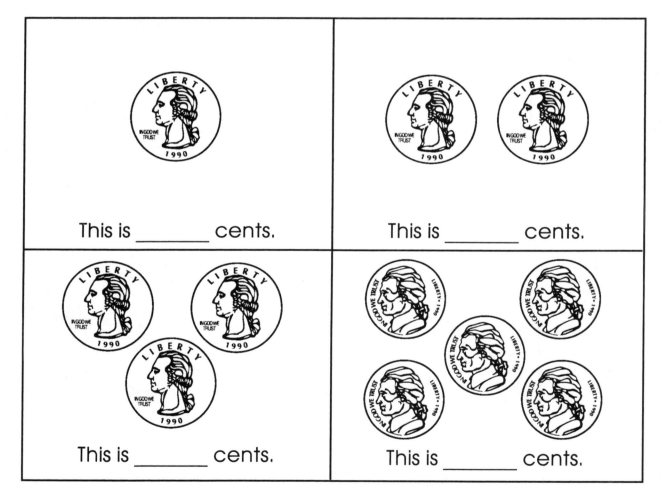

This is _____ cents.

This is _____ cents.

This is _____ cents.

This is _____ cents.

IF87110 *Time & Money*

Dive into Quarters! cont.

Name _____

Mark and Maria found some quarters on their way home from school. They used them to buy apples. How many apples could each buy?

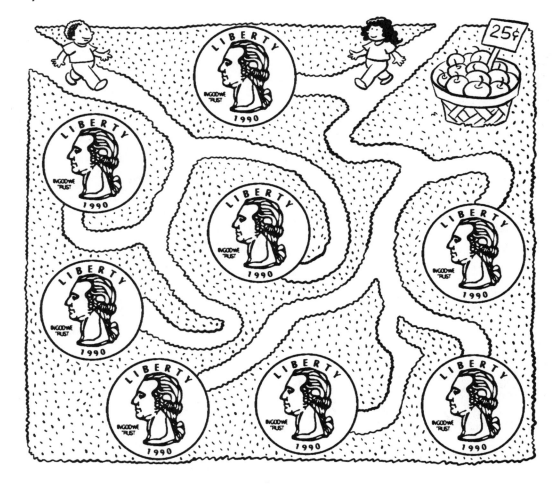

Mark found _____ quarters and bought _____ apples.

Maria found _____ quarters and bought _____ apples.

If you had fifty cents, how many apples could you buy? _____

Name _____

Big Pig Banking!

Count the money in each piggy bank. Then turn it into an addition problem. The first one is done for you.

$$\begin{array}{r} 25¢ \\ +\ 1¢ \\ \hline 26¢ \end{array}$$

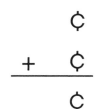

$$\begin{array}{r} ¢ \\ +\quad ¢ \\ \hline ¢ \end{array}$$

$$\begin{array}{r} ¢ \\ +\quad ¢ \\ \hline ¢ \end{array}$$

$$\begin{array}{r} ¢ \\ +\quad ¢ \\ \hline ¢ \end{array}$$

Big Pig Banking! cont.

Name _____

Ç
+   Ç
_____
Ç

Ç
+   Ç
_____
Ç

Let's crack open a piggy
bank and count the money!

Here's what was inside:

2 dimes   **1 nickel**   **4 pennies**

Count the dimes by 10s: _____ Ç

Count the nickels by 5s: _____ Ç

Count the pennies by 1s: _____ Ç

Total: _____ Ç

Could you trade the coins in your bank for three dimes?

Yes   **No**

Name _____

Money Mom

Meet Mrs. Quarter!

The school bell just rang. Help Mrs. Quarter!
Circle each of her kids.

(**Hint:** Each child equals 25¢, just like Mrs. Quarter!)

Money Mom cont.

Name _____

Circle Mrs. Quarter's children.

83

Name _____

Quarters Have Cent Power

Can quarters stand up to whole handfuls of coins? Let's find out! Write >, <, or = in each blank below.

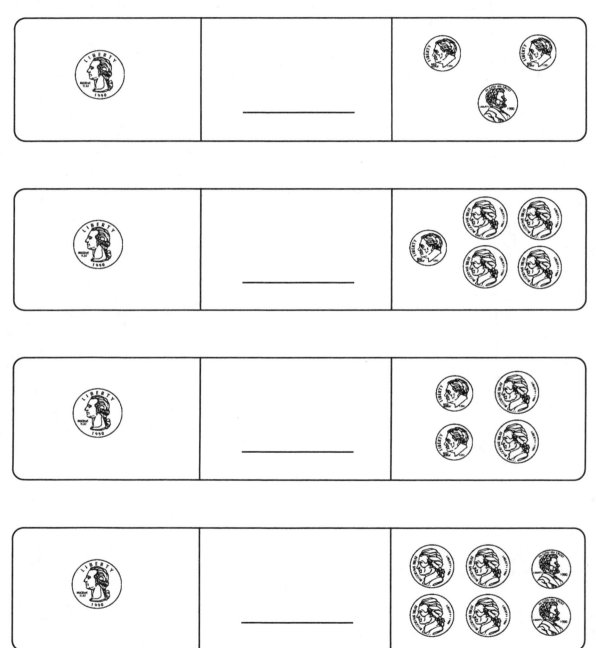

Name _____

Write the value of the coins shown.

Write >, <, or = in each blank.

_____35___¢ _____ _____¢

_____¢ _____ _____¢

_____¢ _____ _____¢

Circle the amounts that are greater than 25¢.

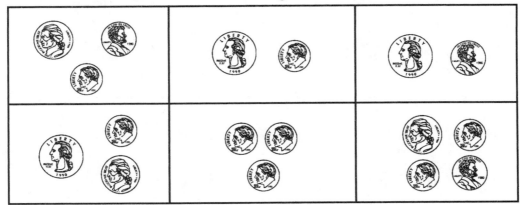

Name _____

All Quarters Are Equal

Right now, most U.S. quarters look like this:

New quarters, with a different picture for each U.S. state, are being *minted*. Minting a coin means stamping it out from metal.

This is the new quarter for the state of Delaware. One side has changed very little. The other side shows Delaware's name and its special state picture.

The quarters with state pictures are worth the same as the old quarters: 25¢. Four quarters = one dollar.

Circle the coins that add up to 25¢.

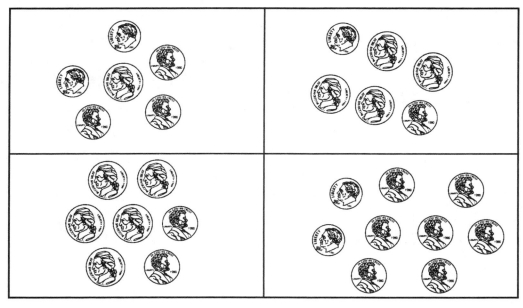

All Quarters are Equal cont.

Name _____

Travel on this path. Each time you add up 25¢, circle the coins that make that amount. Then trade that amount in by crossing out one of the quarters in the box.

Start Here!

**The End!
You made it!**

How many quarters are left over in the box? _____

Name _____

Zooming Down Cents Lane

Add:

8¢
+ 3¢

9¢
+ 7¢

7¢
+ 5¢

6¢
+ 9¢

7¢
+ 6¢

8¢
+ 6¢

9¢
+ 8¢

8¢
+ 7¢

5¢
+ 8¢

8¢
+ 8¢

9¢
+ 9¢

7¢
+ 4¢

6¢
+ 4¢

Name _____

Cents-ible Racing

9¢
+ 5¢

6¢
+ 9¢

4¢
+ 7¢

6¢
+ 7¢

9¢
+ 4¢

5¢
+ 5¢

7¢
+ 9¢

7¢
+ 2¢

5¢
+ 9¢

4¢
+ 8¢

6¢
+ 5¢

7¢
+ 3¢

8¢
+ 2¢

Name _____

Cents at the Park

Subtract:

10¢
− 2¢
———

14¢
− 7¢
———

13¢
− 8¢
———

10¢
− 6¢
———

11¢
− 1¢
———

17¢
− 9¢
———

11¢
− 7¢
———

10¢
− 6¢
———

10¢
− 4¢
———

12¢
− 8¢
———

16¢
− 7¢
———

10¢
− 9¢
———

10¢
− 7¢
———

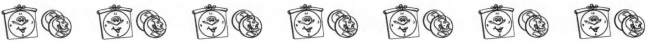

Cents at the Park cont.

Name _____

Subtract:

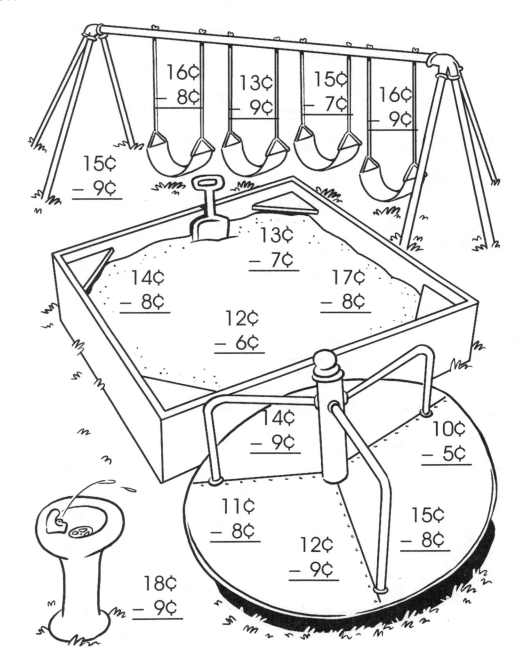

$$16¢ - 8¢$$

$$13¢ - 9¢$$

$$15¢ - 7¢$$

$$16¢ - 9¢$$

$$15¢ - 9¢$$

$$13¢ - 7¢$$

$$14¢ - 8¢$$

$$17¢ - 8¢$$

$$12¢ - 6¢$$

$$14¢ - 9¢$$

$$10¢ - 5¢$$

$$11¢ - 8¢$$

$$12¢ - 9¢$$

$$15¢ - 8¢$$

$$18¢ - 9¢$$

IF87110 *Time & Money*

Name _____

Spending Money Is Subtracting

Billy and his friends went to a yard sale. Subtract the value of the coins shown from the price of each item. This will show how much money each person had left over.

Billy has: He buys: Billy's money:

30¢

☐
− 30¢
─────

Amount left: _____ ¢

Christina has: She buys: Christina's money:

15¢

☐
−   ¢
─────

Amount left: _____ ¢

Name _____

Maria has:　　She buys:　　Maria's money:

42¢

[___]
− _____ ¢

Amount left: _____ ¢

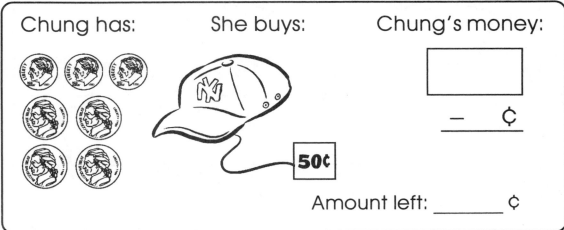

Chung has:　　She buys:　　Chung's money:

50¢

[___]
− _____ ¢

Amount left: _____ ¢

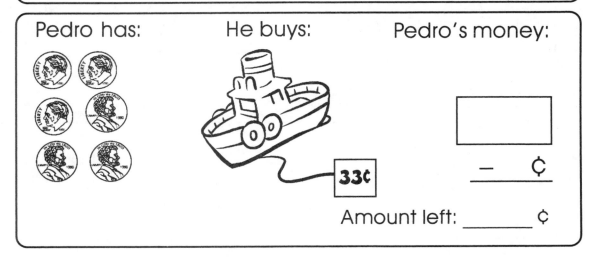

Pedro has:　　He buys:　　Pedro's money:

33¢

[___]
− _____ ¢

Amount left: _____ ¢

Name _____

A Store Story

Pedro and Earl want to open a store! They get ready by adding and subtracting prices.

Add the prices:

1.

2.

3.

A Store Story cont.

Name _____

Help Earl and Pedro practice for their store!
Add or subtract:

1.
$$\begin{array}{r} 39¢ \\ + 21¢ \\ \hline \end{array}$$

2.
$$\begin{array}{r} 26¢ \\ + 44¢ \\ \hline \end{array}$$

3.
$$\begin{array}{r} 55¢ \\ + 26¢ \\ \hline \end{array}$$

4.
$$\begin{array}{r} 45¢ \\ - 26¢ \\ \hline \end{array}$$

5.
$$\begin{array}{r} 24¢ \\ - 18¢ \\ \hline \end{array}$$

6.
$$\begin{array}{r} 81¢ \\ - 49¢ \\ \hline \end{array}$$

7.
$$\begin{array}{r} 71¢ \\ - 59¢ \\ \hline \end{array}$$

8.
$$\begin{array}{r} 62¢ \\ - 58¢ \\ \hline \end{array}$$

9.
$$\begin{array}{r} 34¢ \\ - 26¢ \\ \hline \end{array}$$

A Diller, a Dollar!

Not all money comes in coins. We have paper money, too. Paper money is based on dollars. This is how we write "one dollar": **$1.00**

Ask to look at a real dollar. Look at both sides. Here are small pictures of the front and back of a dollar. Some of the words are not the same as on a real dollar.

A dollar is easier to carry than coins. You would have to carry 100 pennies for 1 dollar!

Practice writing **$1.00** below. All of these amounts equal to one dollar.

100 pennies = _____   20 nickels = _____

10 dimes = _____   4 quarters = _____

If you wanted to carry $1.00 in coins, which would you pick to have the fewest coins in your pocket?

pennies   nickels   dimes   quarters

Name _____

Let's make a dollar sign! Color all the dollar bills **green**. Color all the other kinds of money **brown**.

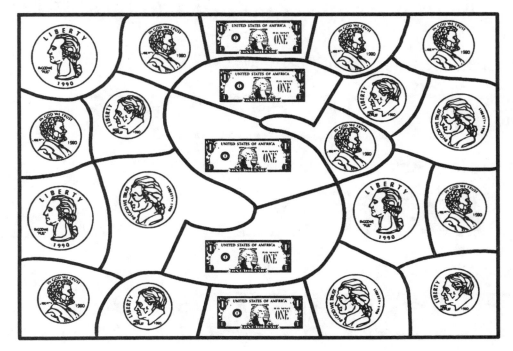

Now write the dollar amounts. The first one is done for you.

$2.00

Name _____

Birthday Surprise

Alesha's birthday was on Sunday. Her whole family was there.

Alesha's grandfather gave her this:

 = _____ dollars

Alesha's brother Kareem gave her this:

 = _____ dollars

Alesha's Uncle Fred gave her this:

 = _____ dollars

Alesha's little sister Ayla gave her this:

 = _____ dollar

Add up all the gifts! How many dollar bills
did Alesha get as birthday gifts? Write the number: _____

We write the dollar
sign here.

This means there
are no added cents.

$ _____ .00

Write the number of
Alesha's dollars here.

Name _____

Now let's help Alesha spend her birthday money! Cross out the number of dollars she spends at each place. Then write how many dollars she has left on the line.

1. First, Alesha goes to the bank. She puts $3.00 in her savings account.
How many dollars does she have left? $ _____ .00 .

2. Then Alesha walks to the toy store. She buys a toy for Ayla.

$1.00

How many dollars does she have left? $ _____ .00 .

3. Alesha stops to buy an ice cream treat.

Today Only!
$1.00

How many dollars does she have left now?

$ _____ .00 .

4. Alesha walks to the pet store to buy three new fish for her fish tank.

$1.00 each

How much money does Alesha have left after all her shopping?

$ _____ .00 .

Name _____

What Is Money?

Money is made of metal. Money is made of paper.
Circle the money made of metal. Put an **X** over the money made of paper.

People earn money by working.

When you buy something, you give away some of your money.
If the ice cream cone costs 75¢, what coins would you use to buy it?

_____ quarters

Name _____

Circle the place where you will need money.

Money has value. Here are some of the coins we have in the United States.

1. Which coin is worth 25¢? **penny** **nickel** **dime** **quarter**

2. Which coin is worth 5¢? **penny** **nickel** **dime** **quarter**

3. Which coin is worth 1¢? **penny** **nickel** **dime** **quarter**

4. Which coin is worth 10¢? **penny** **nickel** **dime** **quarter**

5. Write the number of coins it would take to equal a quarter:

 = _____ dimes + _____ nickels.

OR = _____ nickels

6. Write the number of coins it would take to equal a dime:

 = _____ nickels + _____ pennies

OR = _____ pennies

Name _____

Money on Parade!

Time for a parade! Write the answers in the blanks.

Look at the pennies! We count them by _____ s.

Each penny in the band is worth _____ ¢.

There go the nickels! We count them by _____ s.

Each nickel clown is worth _____ ¢.

Here are the dimes! We count them by _____ s.

Each dime balloon is worth _____ ¢.

Money on Parade! cont.

Name _____

Here come the quarters! They are worth even more! Each quarter wheel is worth _____ ¢.

Look at the dollars! They are paper, not coins. Each dollar flag is worth _____ pennies!

Here is the money from the parade! Draw a line to match each piece of money with its value.

10¢   5¢   1¢   25¢ $1.00

What was your favorite thing in the parade?_____

_____

Name _____

Time Flies

Time moves even when we are asleep. It always moves at the same rate. On some days, time seems to go slowly, but on other days, time flies!

Color the picture from each pair that shows time when it feels fast.

Page 4

Name _____

Color the picture from each pair that shows time when it feels fast.

Page 5

Name _____

Color the picture from each pair that shows the job that would take less time to do.

Page 6

Name _____

Time for Tasks!

Do you help at home? Some chores take more time than others.

Color the picture from each pair that shows the job that would take less time to do.

Page 7

Page 8

Name _____

Meet a Minute!

Have you ever heard someone say, "Just a minute"? What does that mean?

How long is a minute? Let's find out!

Ask an adult to time you. Then count the number of times you do each thing for a whole minute. Write the answer on the line.

I hopped _____ times in one minute.

Answers will vary.

I tapped my shoulder _____ times in one minute.

Page 8

Page 9

Meet a Minute cont.

Name _____

Write your answers on the lines.

I touched my toes _____ times in one minute.

Answers will vary.

I picked up _____ sticks in one minute

I put away _____ toys in one minute.

Page 9

Page 10

Name _____

What Machine Measures Time?

Use these words with the clock to fill in the blanks:

circle	hands	12
face	6	clock

This machine works all day and all night. We never turn it off.

It has a **face** (A), but no eyes and no nose!

It has **hands** (B, C), but no fingers.

The little hand (B) is pointing to **6** .

The big hand (C) is pointing to **12** .

This machine is shaped like a **circle** . (D)

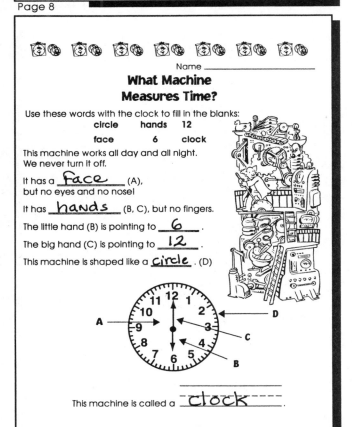

This machine is called a **clock** .

Page 10

Page 11

Name _____

Two Hands to Tell Time

A clock needs two hands to tell us the time.

The big hand is called the minute hand. Find the minute hand and color it **purple**.

The little hand is called the hour hand. Find the hour hand and color it **yellow**.

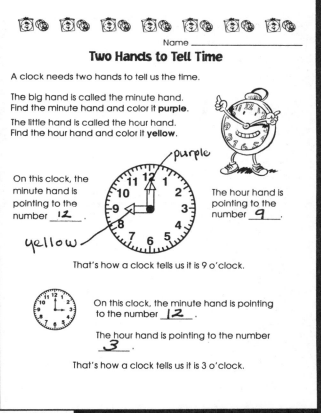

On this clock, the minute hand is pointing to the number **12** .

The hour hand is pointing to the number **9** .

purple

yellow

That's how a clock tells us it is 9 o'clock.

On this clock, the minute hand is pointing to the number **12** .

The hour hand is pointing to the number **3** .

That's how a clock tells us it is 3 o'clock.

Page 11

© Instructional Fair • TS Denison

105

IF87110 *Time & Money*

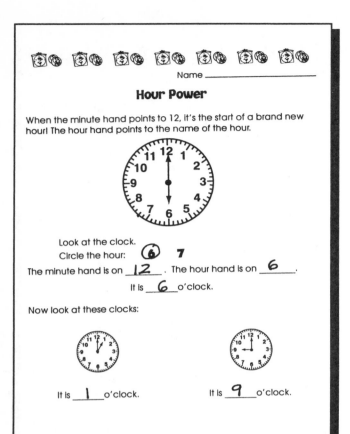

Hour Power

When the minute hand points to 12, it's the start of a brand new hour! The hour hand points to the name of the hour.

Look at the clock.
Circle the hour: ⑥ 7

The minute hand is on __12__. The hour hand is on __6__.

It is __6__ o'clock.

Now look at these clocks:

It is __1__ o'clock.   It is __9__ o'clock.

Page 12

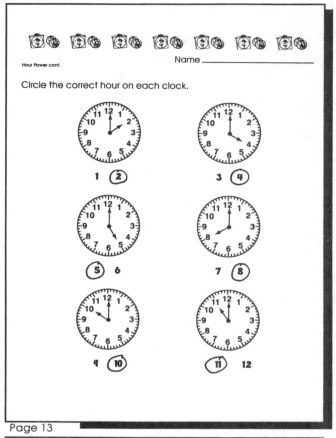

Hour Power cont.

Circle the correct hour on each clock.

1 ②   3 ④

⑤ 6   7 ⑧

9 ⑩   ⑪ 12

Page 13

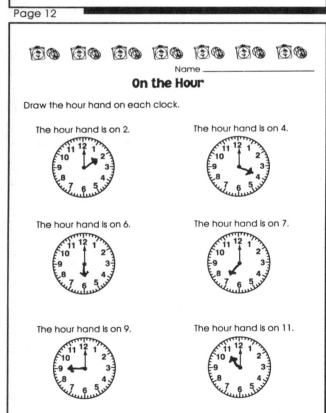

On the Hour

Draw the hour hand on each clock.

The hour hand is on 2.   The hour hand is on 4.

The hour hand is on 6.   The hour hand is on 7.

The hour hand is on 9.   The hour hand is on 11.

Page 14

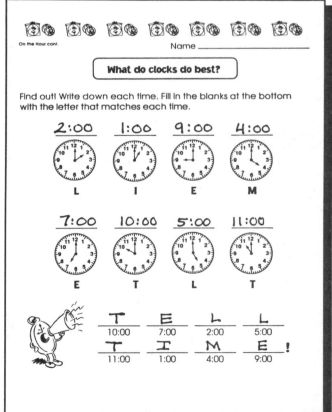

On the Hour cont.

What do clocks do best?

Find out! Write down each time. Fill in the blanks at the bottom with the letter that matches each time.

| 2:00 | 1:00 | 9:00 | 4:00 |
| L | I | E | M |

| 7:00 | 10:00 | 5:00 | 11:00 |
| E | T | L | T |

| T | E | L | L |
| 10:00 | 7:00 | 2:00 | 5:00 |

| T | I | M | E ! |
| 11:00 | 1:00 | 4:00 | 9:00 |

Page 15

Mystery of the Missing Hands

Oh, no! Someone took half the clock hands!

You can help. Draw the missing hand for each clock.

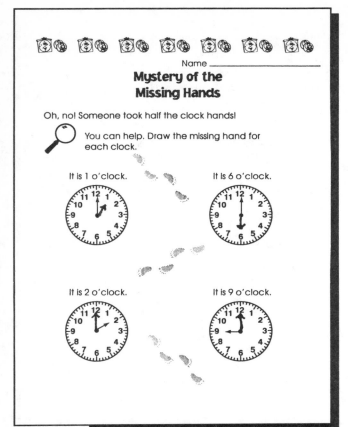

It is 1 o'clock.

It is 6 o'clock.

It is 2 o'clock.

It is 9 o'clock.

Clue: When both the minute and the hour hand are pointing to 12, it is 12:00.

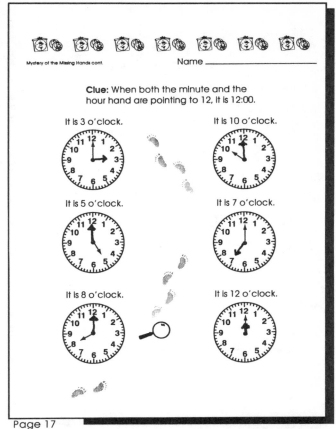

It is 3 o'clock.

It is 10 o'clock.

It is 5 o'clock.

It is 7 o'clock.

It is 8 o'clock.

It is 12 o'clock.

Half the Story!

When the minute hand moves all the way around the clock face, that's one hour. When it moves only halfway, that's a called a half-hour.

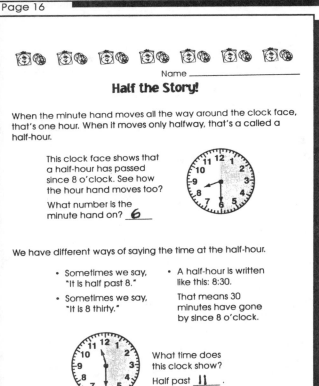

This clock face shows that a half-hour has passed since 8 o'clock. See how the hour hand moves too?

What number is the minute hand on? **6**

We have different ways of saying the time at the half-hour.

- Sometimes we say, "It is half past 8."
- Sometimes we say, "It is 8 thirty."

- A half-hour is written like this: 8:30.

  That means 30 minutes have gone by since 8 o'clock.

What time does this clock show?

Half past **11** .

What time is it?

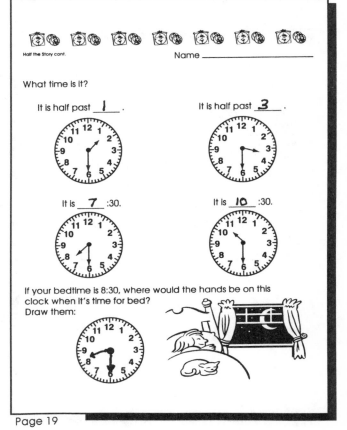

It is half past **1** .

It is half past **3** .

It is **7** :30.

It is **10** :30.

If your bedtime is 8:30, where would the hands be on this clock when it's time for bed? Draw them:

Half-Hour Stories

Can you keep track of the time in these stories?

Mark started a sand castle at 12 o'clock.

Write the time: **12** :00

At half past 12, Mark's mother said, "Lunch time!"

Write the time: **12** :30

Mark put a flag on his castle at 1 o'clock.

Write the time: **1** :00

Half-Hour Stories cont.

Name _____

Draw the clock hands to show times in this story.

Maria and Chung walked to the park at 2 o'clock.

The time is 2:00.

They played on the swings until half past 2.

The time is 2:30.

Chung played on the slide at 3 o'clock.

The time is 3:00.

Maria said, "Let's race home!" They got home at half past 3.

The time is 3:30.

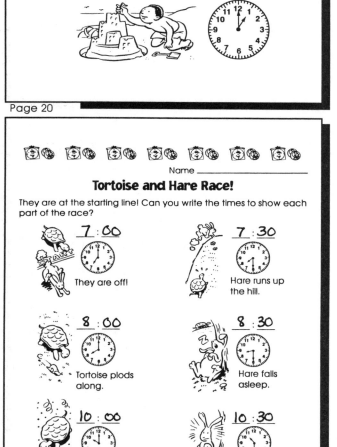

Tortoise and Hare Race!

They are at the starting line! Can you write the times to show each part of the race?

7:**00** — They are off!

7:**30** — Hare runs up the hill.

8:**00** — Tortoise plods along.

8:**30** — Hare falls asleep.

10:**00** — Tortoise crosses the finish line!

10:**30** — Hare wakes up. "Oh, no!"

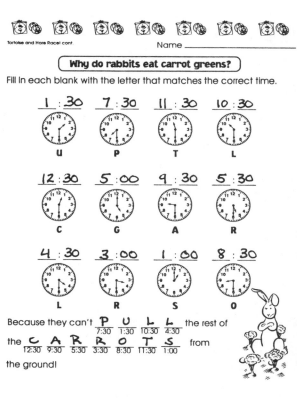

Tortoise and Hare Race! cont.

Name _____

Why do rabbits eat carrot greens?

Fill in each blank with the letter that matches the correct time.

1:30	**7:30**	**11:30**	**10:30**
U	P	T	L

12:30	**5:00**	**9:30**	**5:30**
C	G	A	R

4:30	**3:00**	**1:00**	**8:30**
L	R	S	O

Because they can't **P   U   L   L** the rest of
7:30 1:30 10:30 4:30

the **C   A   R   R   O   T   S** from
12:30 9:30 5:30 3:30 8:30 11:30 1:00

the ground!

Name _____

A Half-Hour = 30 Minutes

Eva practices piano at:
4 : **00**

Pam eats lunch at:
11 : **00**

David does his homework at:
3 : **00**

Earl reads each night at: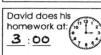
7 : **00**

1. What time does David start his homework?
   3 o'clock

2. If David works for thirty minutes, what time does he finish?
   3:30

3. If Eva plays piano for thirty minutes each day, what time does she stop? **4:30**

4. If Pam has thirty minutes for lunch, what time is lunch over? **11:30**

5. If Earl reads for a half-hour each night, what time does he finish? **7:30**

Name _____

Sam eats lunch at 12:00. Thirty minutes later, he is back in class. What time does lunch end?
12 : **30**

It took Alexa thirty minutes to set up her dolls. She was done at 2:30. What time did she start?
2 : **00**

David made a sand castle. He worked for thirty minutes. He finished at 11:00. What time did he start?
10 : **30**

Martha and her mother bake bread. The bread bakes for thirty minutes. If they put the bread in the oven at 3:30, what time will it be done?
4 : **00**

Name _____

Half of a Half!

There are two half-hours in one hour.

Color one half-hour **red**.   Color the other half-hour **blue**.

How many quarter-hours are in one hour?

Let's find out!

Color one quarter-hour **yellow**.   green
Color one quarter-hour **green**.   yellow
Color one quarter-hour **orange**.
Color one quarter-hour **purple**.   purple
How many quarter-hours did you color?   orange

1   2   3   (4)

   Now draw lines to divide this clock into quarter-hours!

Name _____

Each quarter-hour is 15 minutes. From the 12 to the 3 on a clock is the first quarter-hour.
5 minutes
10 minutes
15 minutes

We say, "It is quarter past 9."
We write it like this: 9:15.

Draw the hands.

5:15
15 minutes after **5** o'clock.

10:15
15 minutes after **10** o'clock.

2:15
15 minutes after **2** o'clock.

9:15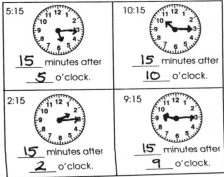
15 minutes after **9** o'clock.

Quarter-Hour Hero

Follow Wonder Worm through a day!

Wonder Worm fixes a bridge!

The time is **7** :15.

Wonder Worm saves a planet!

The time is **8** :15.

Wonder Worm stops a flood!

The time is **11** :15.

Wonder Worm takes time for lunch!

The time is **12** :15.

Quarter-Hour Hero cont.   Name _____

Wonder Worm finds a lost kitten!

The time is **2** :15.

Wonder Worm puts out a fire!

The time is **3** :15.

Wonder Worm is on the news!

The time is **6** :15.

Wonder Worm needs his sleep!

The time is **8** :15.

Draw the hands on the clock:

Wonder Worm's lunch time: **12:15**

Wonder Worm's bedtime: **8:15**

Give Me "Five"!

Do you remember how many minutes are in a half-hour? You can always find out by counting each five-minute space between the clock numbers. Count by 5s to fill in the boxes.

0
5
10
15
20
25
30

Tell the time:

9 : **00**

Five minutes later:

9 : **05**

Start from 12, and count by 5s to see how many minutes past the hour the minute hand has moved.

12 : **26**

10 : **35**

7 : **10**

Give Me "Five"! cont.   Name _____

> **What's the first thing you should do in the morning when you wake up?**

To solve the puzzle, write down each time. Then, fill in the blanks with the letters that match the times. Use the pictures and letters to say the answer out loud!

9 : **15**   **9** : **00**   **9** : **25**   **9** : **20**

A   n   c   L

9 : **30**   **9** : **05**   **9** : **20**   **9** : **35**

S   T   L   !

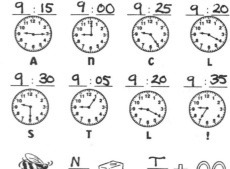

$\dfrac{N}{9:00}$ $\dfrac{T}{9:05}$ + OO

$\dfrac{A}{9:15}$ $\dfrac{L}{9:20}$ $\dfrac{C}{9:25}$ $\dfrac{S}{9:30}$ $\dfrac{!}{9:35}$

Be **Nice to alarm clocks!**

IF87110 Time & Money

Halfway Around the Clock

Name _____

There are five minutes between each number on the face of a clock... so count by 5s to count halfway around!

5 minutes
10 minutes
15 minutes
20 minutes
25 minutes
30 minutes

When you count halfway around the clock, that's a half-hour!

A half-hour is __30__ minutes.

What time does this clock say? __8__ : __00__

Now show the time 30 minutes later. Draw the hands.

Halfway Around the Clock cont.

Name _____

Travel the paths. Match each clock with the time a half-hour later.

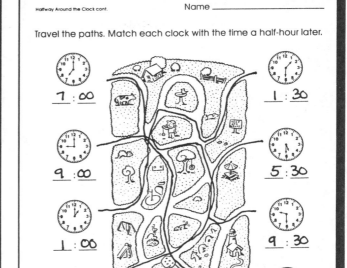

__7__ : __00__

__9__ : __00__

__1__ : __00__

__5__ : __00__

__1__ : __30__

__5__ : __30__

__9__ : __30__

__7__ : __30__

What a Time with Chiggles

Name _____

Fill in the blanks with the correct times. Then write the letter for each time in the correct space on page 35, in the story about David's new puppy, Chiggles.

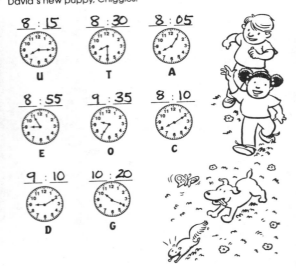

__8__ : __15__   __8__ : __30__   __8__ : __05__
      U   T   A

__8__ : __55__   __9__ : __35__   __8__ : __10__
      E   O   C

__9__ : __10__   __10__ : __20__
      D   G

What a Time with Chiggles cont.

Name _____

What a day! Dad came home with Chiggles, our new puppy, at 8:05 __A__ . She has a big wet nose and floppy ears. Dad said at 8:10 __C__ that I could take her for a walk.

At 8:15, __U__ the phone rang. It was Alesha. She wanted to meet Chiggles right away.

Alesha came over at 8:30 __T__ . I showed her my new friend!

Alesha and I played with Chiggles. Then we saw that it was 8:55 __E__ . Five minutes later, we took our walk to the park on that sunny, warm day.

By 9:10 __D__ , Chiggles was chasing butterflies and squirrels. Lots of people stopped to pet Chiggles. We got home at 9:35 __O__ .

Alesha went home. Then I sat on the porch swing, holding my puppy. Chiggles fell asleep with her nose against my neck. The clock said 10:20 __G__ . That's the last thing I remember, because I fell asleep, too!

Write the letters from the blanks on page 34 in order to see what Chiggles will be when she grows up:

__A__ __C__ __U__ __T__ __E__ __D__ __O__ __G__!

111

What a Mess!

Help clean up the clock room. Write down each time. Then number the row of clocks from 1 to 3, with 1 as the earliest time. Write **1**, **2**, or **3** in each box.

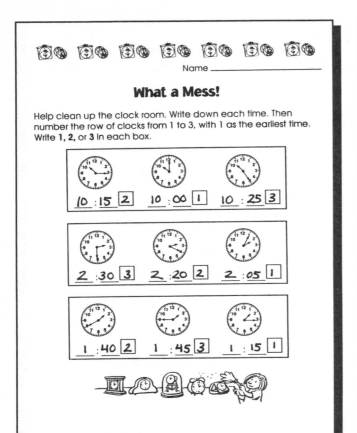

10 : 15 [2]   10 : 00 [1]   10 : 25 [3]

2 : 30 [3]   2 : 20 [2]   2 : 05 [1]

1 : 40 [2]   1 : 45 [3]   1 : 15 [1]

Write each time. Then write **1**, **2**, or **3** in each box, with 1 being the earliest time.

2 : 00 [1]   2 : 35 [3]   2 : 20 [2]

6 : 15 [3]   6 : 10 [2]   6 : 05 [1]

12 : 30 [2]   12 : 15 [1]   12 : 40 [3]

All Kinds of Clocks

Clocks tell us the time,
No matter how it flies.
A clock will show the time for bed,
And when the sun will rise.

Clocks tell the time for breakfast,
And lunch and dinner too.
What times of day, of work and play,
Are these clocks telling you?

There are all kinds of clocks. Circle the ones you have seen.

Answers will vary.

Dial clocks look like this:

Digital clocks look like this: [2:45]

If you have a watch, is it dial or digital?
Circle the correct picture: **Answers will vary.**

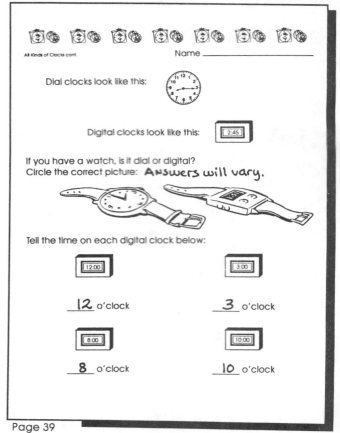

Tell the time on each digital clock below:

[12:00]   [3:00]

__12__ o'clock   __3__ o'clock

[8:00]   [10:00]

__8__ o'clock   __10__ o'clock

Reading Time

Name _____

On a dial clock, you look at the hands to read the time.

It is **6** o'clock.

On a digital clock, the numbers say the time.

6:00 — These are the minutes. When they are both zero, you say "o'clock."

This is the hour.

When a digital clock shows quarter hours and half hours, it shows them as minutes.

A quarter-hour is **15** minutes. This is the same time as "It is a quarter past **6**." **6:15**

A half-hour is **30** minutes.
This is the time, "It is half-past **4**." **4:30**

Write the times in the digital faces.

1. **2:30** "It is half-past two."
2. **11:15** "It is quarter past eleven."
3. **3:00** "It is 3 o'clock."

Reading Time cont.

Name _____

Draw a line to each matching time.

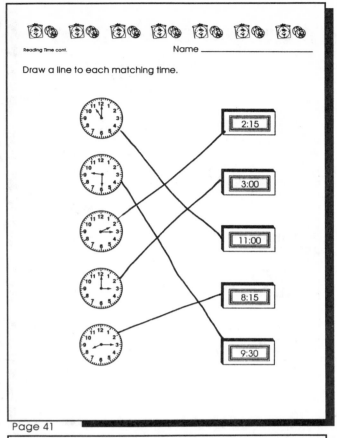

2:15
3:00
11:00
8:15
9:30

What's the Time?

Name _____

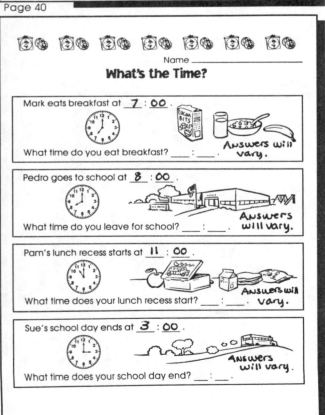

Mark eats breakfast at **7 : 00**.
What time do you eat breakfast? ___ : ___. Answers will vary.

Pedro goes to school at **8 : 00**.
What time do you leave for school? ___ : ___. Answers will vary.

Pam's lunch recess starts at **11 : 00**.
What time does your lunch recess start? ___ : ___. Answers will vary.

Sue's school day ends at **3 : 00**.
What time does your school day end? ___ : ___. Answers will vary.

What's the Time cont.

Name _____

Circle the clock that best answers each question.

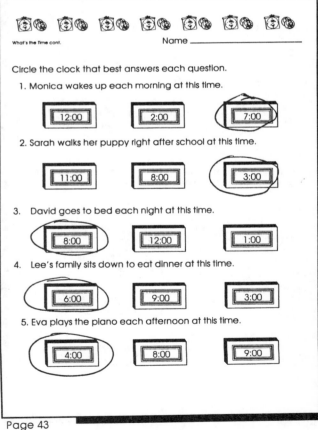

1. Monica wakes up each morning at this time.
   12:00   2:00   (7:00)

2. Sarah walks her puppy right after school at this time.
   11:00   8:00   (3:00)

3. David goes to bed each night at this time.
   (8:00)   12:00   1:00

4. Lee's family sits down to eat dinner at this time.
   (6:00)   9:00   3:00

5. Eva plays the piano each afternoon at this time.
   (4:00)   8:00   9:00

Let's Play with Days!

Name _____

How long is a day? One day is 24 hours long!

You can do many things in one day.

Can you do all these things in one day?
Circle **yes** or **no** at the bottom of the page.

(Yes) no

Now color the pictures!

Page 44

Let's Play with Days! cont.

Name _____

You have a name. So does each day.

Ask an adult to read you the names of the days. Then look at the pictures. Draw a line from each picture to the day when that might happen.

Answers will vary.

Sunday	Monday	Tuesday	Wednesday	Thursday	Friday	Saturday
1	2	3	4	5	6	7

What is your favorite day? Color its square in your favorite color!

Write its name here.

_____
_____

Page 45

Name _____

Working with Weeks

Here is one week on a calendar. Count the days:

Sunday	Monday	Tuesday	Wednesday	Thursday	Friday	Saturday
1	2	3	4	5	6	7

How many days are there in one week?   1   3   5   (7)

Here are the days of the week. Write the number of each day in the blank to show its correct order. Start with Sunday as 1.

Monday **2**

Saturday **7**

Thursday **5**

Tuesday **3**

Sunday **1**

Friday **6**

Wednesday **4**

Page 46

Working with Weeks cont.

Name _____

Let's rocket through a week! Work through the maze by going from one day of the week to the next, in order.

Page 47

Name _____

My Favorite Month

Days and weeks turn into **months**. Most months have 30 or 31 days. Here are all the months in one year! Count them.

How many months in a year? __12__ Now number the months in order, starting with January as **1**.

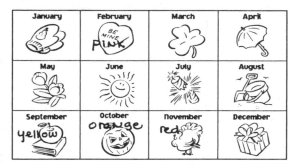

Name _____

Calendar Clues

A calendar counts days and months, just like a clock counts minutes and hours.

Here are the months on a calendar:

January	February	March	April
	BE MINE **PINK**		
May	June	July	August
September	October	November	December
yellow	**orange**	**red**	

What month does school start 🍎? Color that month **yellow**!

In what month is Valentine's Day 💝? Color that month **pink**!

In what month is Halloween 🎃? Color that month **orange**!

In what month is Thanksgiving 🦃? Color that month **red**!

Name _____

Now You Know Time!

hour   half-hour   quarter-hour

Circle the correct numbers.

How many minutes in an hour?   15   30   **60**

How many minutes in a half-hour?   15   **30**   60

How many minutes in a quarter-hour? **15**   30   60

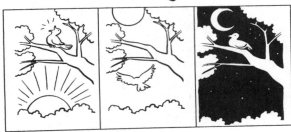

How many hours in a day?   6   12   **24**   48

Now You Know Time I cont.   Name _____

Sunday	Monday	Tuesday	Wednesday	Thursday	Friday	Saturday
1	2	3	4	5	6	7

What day comes after Monday? __Tuesday__

What day comes before Friday? __Thursday__

What day comes between Tuesday and Thursday? __Wednesday__

How many days in a week?   2   4   6   **7**   8   9

January	February	March	April
	BE MINE		
May	June	July	August
September	October	November	December

What month comes before May? __April__

What month comes after December? __January__

How many months in a year?   3   6   8   **12**

IF87110 *Time & Money*

Name _____

One Wonderful Penny

Yes, I'm a penny!
Count me by ones,
And when you are done,
You can spend me,
Or lend me,
Or buy bubblegum!

This is a **penny**.

Ask for a real penny, and lay it on the pictures.
Look at both sides of the penny.

A penny is worth 1 cent, so we count pennies by ones.

Count the pennies. Then write how many on the line.

This is _3_ cents.   This is _5_ cents.

One Wonderful Penny cont.

Name _____

Circle the correct amount of pennies.

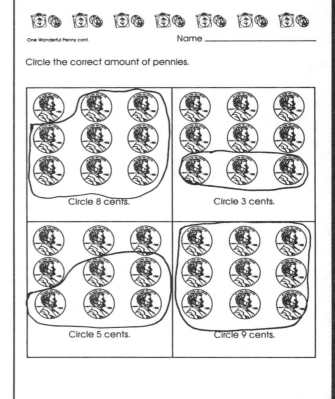

Circle 8 cents.   Circle 3 cents.

Circle 5 cents.   Circle 9 cents.

Name _____

Pennies Add Up!

Find the pennies in each picture. Add them up.

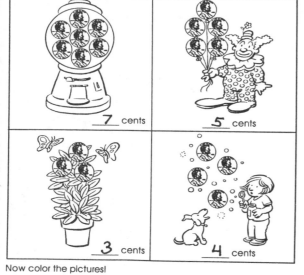

_7_ cents   _5_ cents

_3_ cents   _4_ cents

Now color the pictures!

Name _____

More Pennies to Add!

Add the pennies in each picture.

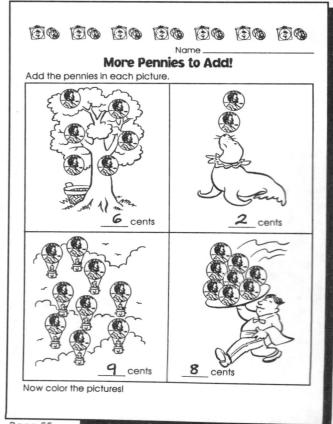

_6_ cents   _2_ cents

_9_ cents   _8_ cents

Now color the pictures!

IF87110 Time & Money

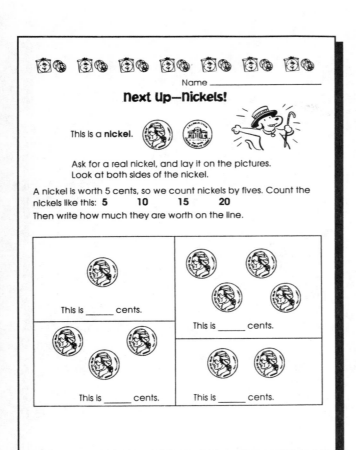

Next Up—Nickels!

This is a **nickel**.

Ask for a real nickel, and lay it on the pictures.
Look at both sides of the nickel.

A nickel is worth 5 cents, so we count nickels by fives. Count the
nickels like this: **5   10   15   20**

Then write how much they are worth on the line.

This is _____ cents.

This is _____ cents.

This is _____ cents.

This is _____ cents.

Name _____

Circle the correct amount of the nickels.

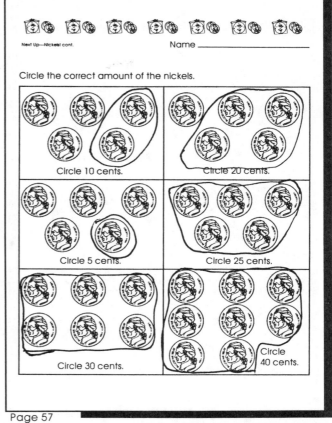

Circle 10 cents.

Circle 20 cents.

Circle 5 cents.

Circle 25 cents.

Circle 30 cents.

Circle 40 cents.

Toy Trade

Let's take nickels to the school toy trade!

Count the nickels. How many do you have?

You have **10** nickels. That's 50 cents!

Put **X**s through the nickels you spend for each toy.

5 CENTS

25 CENTS

Name _____

Put **X**s through the nickels you spend.

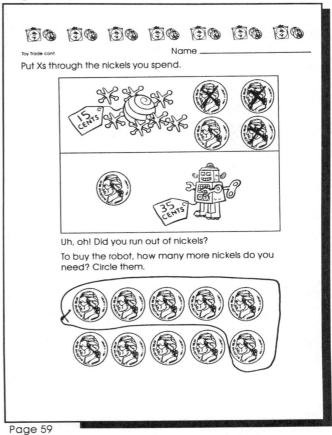

15 CENTS

35 CENTS

Uh, oh! Did you run out of nickels?

To buy the robot, how many more nickels do you
need? Circle them.

Making Cents

One penny is 1 cent. We write 1 cent like this: **1¢**

Color all the shapes with pennies and nickels **blue**.

Color all the other shapes **red**.

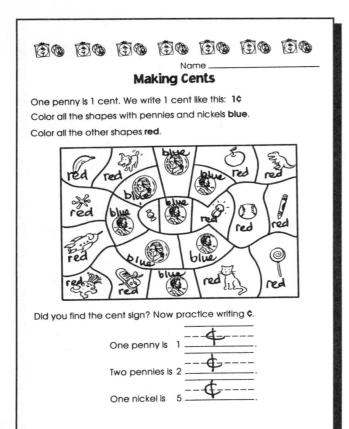

Did you find the cent sign? Now practice writing ¢.

One penny is 1 ___¢___ .

Two pennies is 2 ___¢___ .

One nickel is 5 ___¢___ .

Look at each group of money. Write the amount in cents. The first one is done for you.

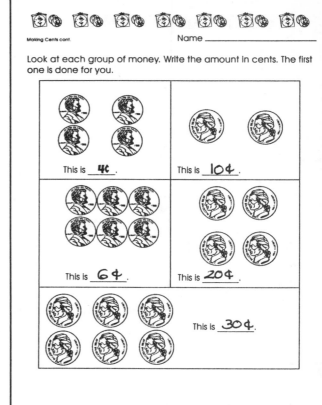

This is __4¢__ . This is __10¢__ .

This is __6¢__ . This is __20¢__ .

This is __30¢__ .

Want to Munch Some Lunch?

Lunch money jingles when
you walk down the hall.
Its bright, ringing sound is
a time-for-lunch call.
What will you buy?
What will you munch?
It depends on the money you
have to buy lunch!

Circle each food choice after you count your money.

Pick something to drink!

You have:

That's __15__ ¢.

20¢   15¢   25¢

Pick your main course!

You have:

That's __30__ ¢.

40¢   30¢   35¢

Circle each food choice after you count your money.

Pick a fruit or vegetable!

You have:

That's __25__ ¢.

25¢   30¢   35¢

Pick a dessert!

You have:

That's __10__ ¢.

25¢   10¢   20¢

Hey! You find this coin in your pocket.

What can you buy with it?
Circle the treat
you can buy.

20¢   5¢   15¢

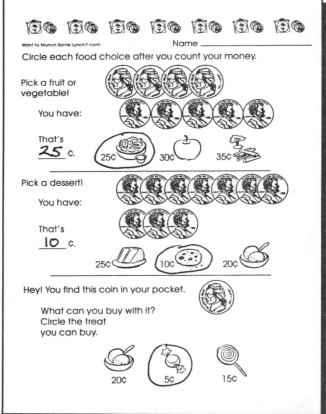

Name _____

Dimes on Deck

This is a **dime**. Ask for a real dime, and lay it on the pictures. Look at both sides of the dime.

A dime is worth 10 cents, so we count dimes by tens. Like this:

10   20   30   40

Count the dimes in each box. Then write the total on each line.

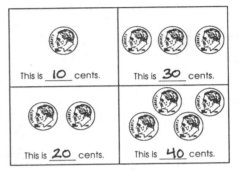

| This is __10__ cents. | This is __30__ cents. |
| This is __20__ cents. | This is __40__ cents. |

Circle the correct number of dimes.

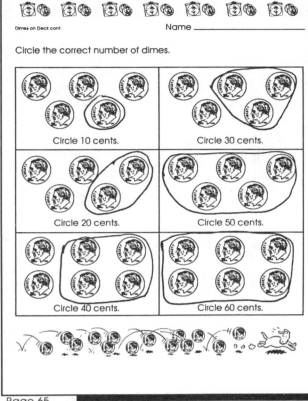

Circle 10 cents.   Circle 30 cents.

Circle 20 cents.   Circle 50 cents.

Circle 40 cents.   Circle 60 cents.

Name _____

A Dime at a Time

Count the dimes. Write the amount in cents. The first one is done for you.

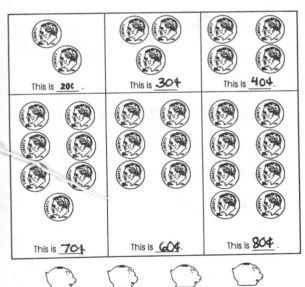

| This is **20¢** . | This is __30¢__ | This is __40¢__ . |
| This is __70¢__ | This is __60¢__ . | This is __80¢__ . |

Count the dimes in each box. Write the totals in cents.

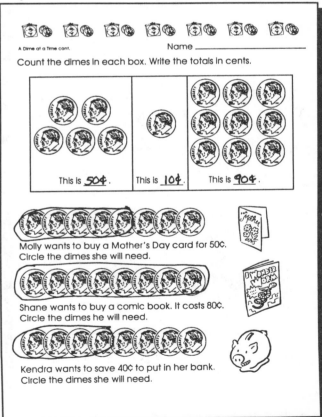

| This is __50¢__ . | This is __10¢__ | This is __90¢__ . |

Molly wants to buy a Mother's Day card for 50¢. Circle the dimes she will need.

Shane wants to buy a comic book. It costs 80¢. Circle the dimes he will need.

Kendra wants to save 40¢ to put in her bank. Circle the dimes she will need.

Birthday Buying

Alexa, Sam, and Mark are all going to Kim's birthday party. Help them buy presents. Draw **X**s through the money they need to buy each gift.

1.

2.

3.

Draw **X**s through the money needed to buy each gift.

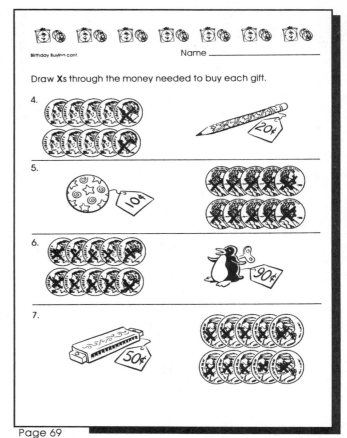

4.

5.

6.

7.

Can It Be Done?

Mrs. Fox's students want to buy her a baby gift. Each student needs to bring in 35 cents. Draw **X**s through each student's coins to equal 35 cents.

1.   Here is Maria's money.

2.   Here is Chung's money.

3.   Here is Alexa's money.

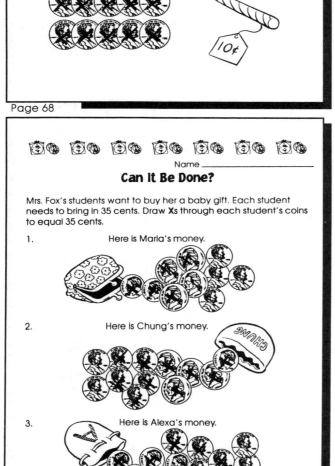

Draw **X**s through each student's coins to equal 35 cents.

4. Here is Kim's money.

5. Here is Sam's money.

6. Here is Kendra's money.

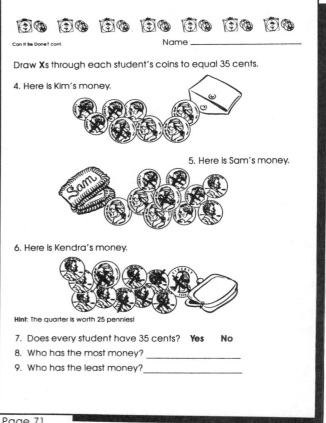

Hint: The quarter is worth 25 pennies!

7. Does every student have 35 cents?   **Yes   No**

8. Who has the most money? _____

9. Who has the least money? _____

       IF87110 *Time & Money*

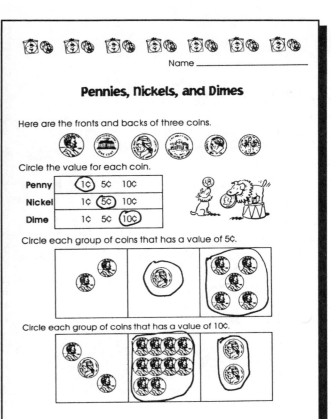

Pennies, Nickels, and Dimes

Here are the fronts and backs of three coins.

Circle the value for each coin.

Penny	(1¢)	5¢	10¢
Nickel	1¢	(5¢)	10¢
Dime	1¢	5¢	(10¢)

Circle each group of coins that has a value of 5¢.

Circle each group of coins that has a value of 10¢.

Page 72

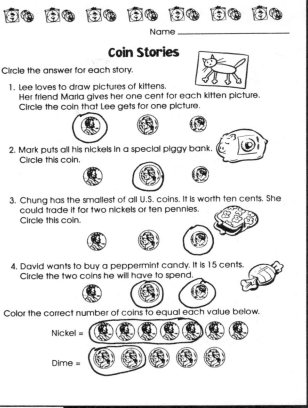

Coin Stories

Circle the answer for each story.

1. Lee loves to draw pictures of kittens. Her friend Maria gives her one cent for each kitten picture. Circle the coin that Lee gets for one picture.

2. Mark puts all his nickels in a special piggy bank. Circle this coin.

3. Chung has the smallest of all U.S. coins. It is worth ten cents. She could trade it for two nickels or ten pennies. Circle this coin.

4. David wants to buy a peppermint candy. It is 15 cents. Circle the two coins he will have to spend.

Color the correct number of coins to equal each value below.

Nickel =

Dime =

Page 73

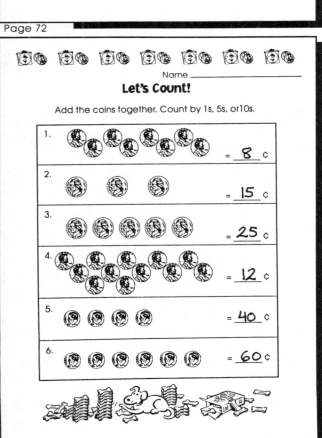

Let's Count!

Add the coins together. Count by 1s, 5s, or 10s.

1.	= 8 ¢
2.	= 15 ¢
3.	= 25 ¢
4.	= 12 ¢
5.	= 40 ¢
6.	= 60 ¢

Page 74

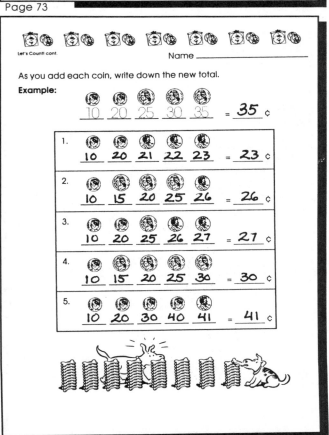

Let's Count! cont.

As you add each coin, write down the new total.

Example:
10 20 25 30 35 = **35** ¢

1.	10 20 21 22 23	= 23 ¢
2.	10 15 20 25 26	= 26 ¢
3.	10 20 25 26 27	= 27 ¢
4.	10 15 20 25 30	= 30 ¢
5.	10 20 30 40 41	= 41 ¢

Page 75

Subtract the value of the coins from the total to find the mystery coin.

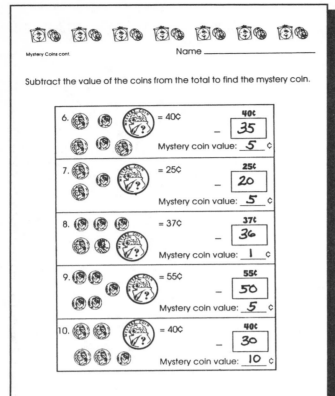

6. = 40¢

40¢
− 35

Mystery coin value: 5 ¢

7. = 25¢

25¢
20

Mystery coin value: 5 ¢

8. = 37¢

37¢
36

Mystery coin value: 1 ¢

9. = 55¢

55¢
50

Mystery coin value: 5 ¢

10. = 40¢

40¢
30

Mystery coin value: 10 ¢

Mystery Coins

Find each mystery coin. Count the coins shown. Subtract that amount from the total shown.

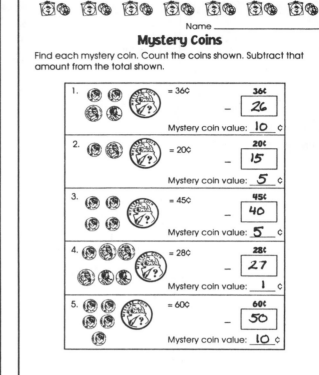

1. = 36¢

36¢
− 26

Mystery coin value: 10 ¢

2. = 20¢

20¢
15

Mystery coin value: 5 ¢

3. = 45¢

45¢
40

Mystery coin value: 5 ¢

4. = 28¢

28¢
27

Mystery coin value: 1 ¢

5. = 60¢

60¢
50

Mystery coin value: 10 ¢

Dive into Quarters!

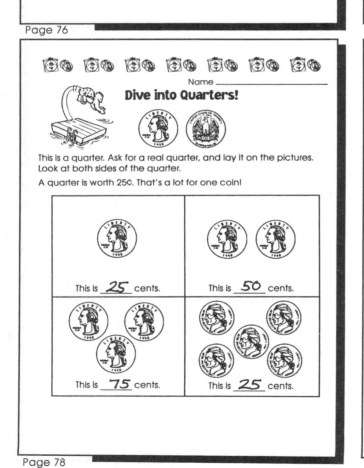

This is a quarter. Ask for a real quarter, and lay it on the pictures. Look at both sides of the quarter.

A quarter is worth 25¢. That's a lot for one coin!

This is 25 cents.   This is 50 cents.

This is 75 cents.   This is 25 cents.

Mark and Marla found some quarters on their way home from school. They used them to buy apples. How many apples could each buy?

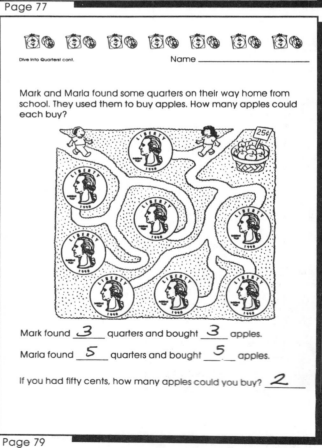

Mark found 3 quarters and bought 3 apples.

Marla found 5 quarters and bought 5 apples.

If you had fifty cents, how many apples could you buy? 2

Big Pig Banking!

Count the money in each piggy bank. Then turn it into an addition problem. The first one is done for you.

Name _____

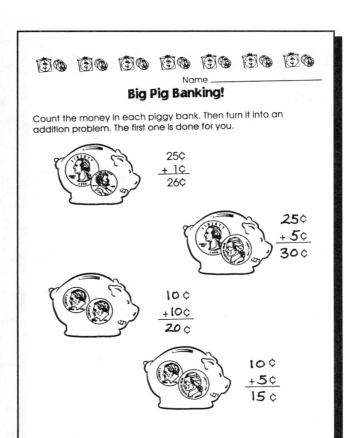

$$25¢$$
$$+ 1¢$$
$$26¢$$

$$25¢$$
$$+ 5¢$$
$$30¢$$

$$10¢$$
$$+10¢$$
$$20¢$$

$$10¢$$
$$+ 5¢$$
$$15¢$$

Name _____

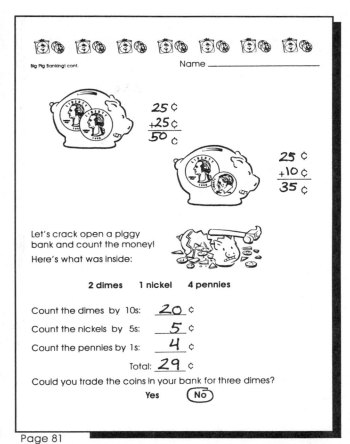

$$25¢$$
$$+25¢$$
$$50¢$$

$$25¢$$
$$+10¢$$
$$35¢$$

Let's crack open a piggy bank and count the money!

Here's what was inside:

2 dimes   1 nickel   4 pennies

Count the dimes by 10s: __20__ ¢

Count the nickels by 5s: __5__ ¢

Count the pennies by 1s: __4__ ¢

Total: __29__ ¢

Could you trade the coins in your bank for three dimes?

Yes   (No)

Money Mom

Name _____

Meet Mrs. Quarter!

The school bell just rang. Help Mrs. Quarter!
Circle each of her kids.

(**Hint:** Each child equals 25¢, just like Mrs. Quarter!)

Name _____

Circle Mrs. Quarter's children.

Quarters Have Cent Power

Can quarters stand up to whole handfuls of coins? Let's find out! Write
>, <, or = in each blank below.

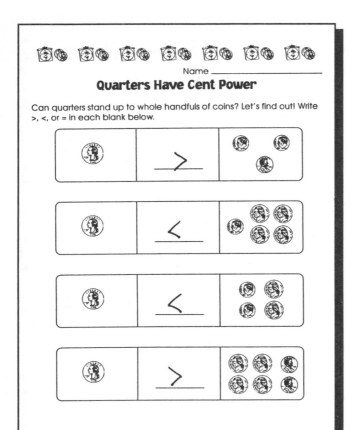

Write the value of the coins shown.

Write >, <, or = in each center blank.

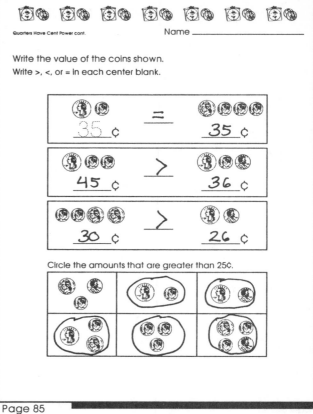

Circle the amounts that are greater than 25¢.

All Quarters Are Equal

Right now, most U.S. quarters look like this:

New quarters, with a different picture
for each U.S. state, are being *minted*.
Minting a coin means stamping it out
from metal.

This is the new quarter for the
state of Delaware. One side has
changed very little. The other side
shows Delaware's name and its
special state picture.

The quarters with state pictures are worth the same as the old quarters:
25¢. Four quarters = one dollar.

Circle the coins that add up to 25¢.

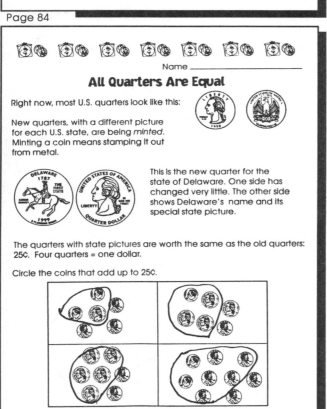

Travel on this path. Each time you
add up 25¢, circle the coins that
make that amount. Then trade
that amount in by crossing out
one of the quarters in the box.

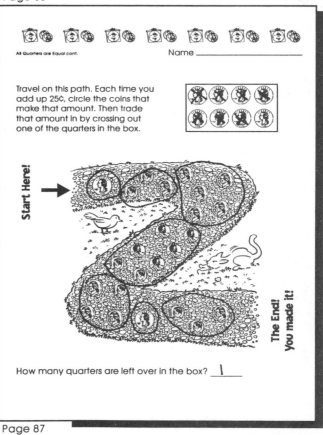

How many quarters are left over in the box? ___1___

Page 84

Page 85

Page 86

Page 87

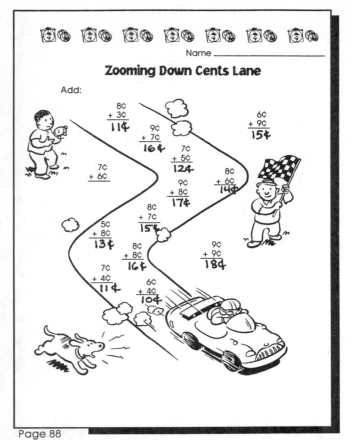

Name _____

Zooming Down Cents Lane

Add:

$$8¢ + 3¢ = 11¢$$
$$9¢ + 7¢ = 16¢$$
$$6¢ + 9¢ = 15¢$$
$$7¢ + 5¢ = 12¢$$
$$7¢ + 6¢$$
$$8¢ + 6¢ = 14¢$$
$$9¢ + 8¢ = 17¢$$
$$8¢ + 7¢ = 15¢$$
$$5¢ + 8¢ = 13¢$$
$$8¢ + 8¢ = 16¢$$
$$9¢ + 9¢ = 18¢$$
$$7¢ + 4¢ = 11¢$$
$$6¢ + 4¢ = 10¢$$

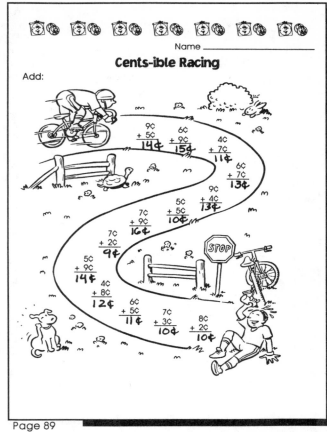

Name _____

Cents-ible Racing

Add:

$$9¢ + 5¢ = 14¢$$
$$6¢ + 9¢ = 15¢$$
$$4¢ + 7¢ = 11¢$$
$$6¢ + 7¢ = 13¢$$
$$9¢ + 4¢ = 13¢$$
$$5¢ + 5¢ = 10¢$$
$$7¢ + 9¢ = 16¢$$
$$7¢ + 2¢ = 9¢$$
$$5¢ + 9¢ = 14¢$$
$$5¢ + 8¢ = 12¢$$
$$6¢ + 5¢ = 11¢$$
$$7¢ + 3¢ = 10¢$$
$$8¢ + 2¢ = 10¢$$

Name _____

Cents at the Park

Subtract:

$$10¢ - 2¢ = 8¢$$
$$14¢ - 7¢ = 7¢$$
$$13¢ - 8¢ = 5¢$$
$$10¢ - 6¢ = 4¢$$
$$11¢ - 7¢ = 4¢$$
$$11¢ - 1¢ = 10¢$$
$$17¢ - 9¢ = 8¢$$
$$10¢ - 6¢ = 4¢$$
$$10¢ - 4¢ = 6¢$$
$$12¢ - 8¢ = 4¢$$
$$16¢ - 7¢ = 9¢$$
$$10¢ - 9¢ = 1¢$$
$$10¢ - 7¢ = 3¢$$

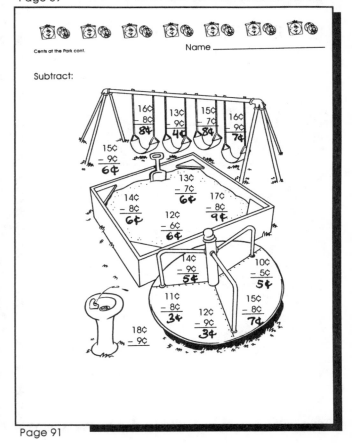

Cents at the Park cont.

Name _____

Subtract:

$$16¢ - 8¢ = 8¢$$
$$13¢ - 9¢ = 4¢$$
$$15¢ - 7¢ = 8¢$$
$$16¢ - 9¢ = 7¢$$
$$15¢ - 9¢ = 6¢$$
$$14¢ - 8¢ = 6¢$$
$$13¢ - 7¢ = 6¢$$
$$17¢ - 8¢ = 9¢$$
$$12¢ - 6¢ = 6¢$$
$$10¢ - 5¢ = 5¢$$
$$14¢ - 9¢ = 5¢$$
$$11¢ - 8¢ = 3¢$$
$$12¢ - 9¢ = 3¢$$
$$15¢ - 8¢ = 7¢$$
$$18¢ - 9¢ =$$

IF87110 *Time & Money*

Spending Money Is Subtracting

Billy and his friends went to a yard sale. Subtract the value of the coins shown from the price of each item. This will show how much money each person had left over.

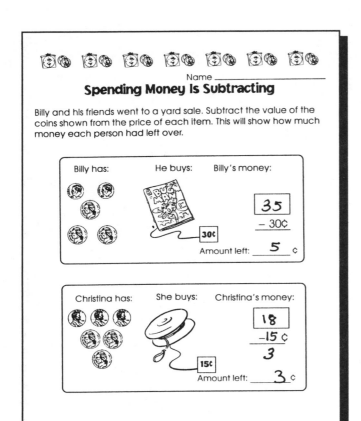

Billy has: He buys: Billy's money:

$$35$$
$$- 30¢$$

Amount left: __5__ ¢

Christina has: She buys: Christina's money:

$$18$$
$$-15¢$$
$$3$$

Amount left: __3__ ¢

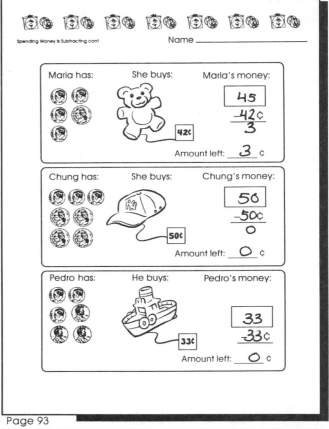

Maria has: She buys: Maria's money:

$$45$$
$$-42¢$$
$$3$$

Amount left: __3__ ¢

Chung has: She buys: Chung's money:

$$50$$
$$-50¢$$
$$0$$

Amount left: __O__ ¢

Pedro has: He buys: Pedro's money:

$$33$$
$$-33¢$$

Amount left: __O__ ¢

Page 93

A Store Story

Pedro and Earl want to open a store! They get ready by adding and subtracting prices.

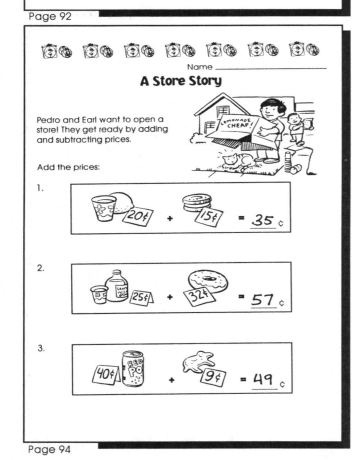

Add the prices:

1. [20¢] + [15¢] = __35__ ¢

2. [25¢] + [32¢] = __57__ ¢

3. [40¢] + [9¢] = __49__ ¢

Page 94

Help Earl and Pedro practice for their store!
Add or subtract:

1.	2.	3.
39¢ + 21¢ **60¢**	26¢ + 44¢ **70¢**	55¢ + 26¢ **81¢**

4.	5.	6.
45¢ − 26¢ **19¢**	24¢ − 18¢ **42¢**	81¢ − 49¢ **32¢**

7.	8.	9.
71¢ − 59¢ **12¢**	62¢ − 58¢ **4¢**	34¢ − 26¢ **8¢**

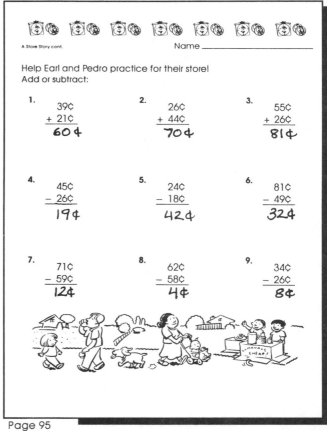

Page 95

A Diller; a Dollar!

Not all money comes in coins. We have paper money, too. Paper money is based on dollars. This is how we write "one dollar": **$1.00**

Ask to look at a real dollar. Look at both sides. Here are small pictures of the front and back of a dollar. Some of the words are not the same as on a real dollar.

A dollar is easier to carry than coins. You would have to carry 100 pennies for 1 dollar!

Practice writing **$1.00** below. All of these amounts equal to one dollar.

100 pennies = $1.00   20 nickels = $1.00

10 dimes = $1.00   4 quarters = $1.00

If you wanted to carry $1.00 in coins, which would you pick to have the fewest coins in your pocket?

pennies   nickels   dimes   (quarters)

A Diller, a Dollar! cont.

Let's make a dollar sign! Color all the dollar bills **green**. Color all the other kinds of money **brown**.

Now write the dollar amounts. The first one is done for you.

 $2.00

 $5.00

 $3.00

     $6.00

Birthday Surprise

Alesha's birthday was on Sunday. Her whole family was there.

Alesha's grandfather gave her this:

= __4__ dollars

Alesha's brother Kareem gave her this:

= __2__ dollars

Alesha's Uncle Fred gave her this:

= __3__ dollars

Alesha's little sister Ayla gave her this:

= __1__ dollar

Add up all the gifts! How many dollar bills did Alesha get as birthday gifts? Write the number: __10__

We write the dollar sign here → $ __10__ .00   This means there are no added cents.

Write the number of Alesha's dollars here.

Birthday Surprise cont.

Now let's help Alesha spend her birthday money! Cross out the number of dollars she spends at each place. Then write how many dollars she has left on the line.

1. First, Alesha goes to the bank. She puts $3.00 in her savings account.
How many dollars does she have left? $ __7__ .00 .

2. Then Alesha walks to the toy store. She buys a toy for Ayla.

How many dollars does she have left? $ __6__ .00 .

3. Alesha stops to buy an ice cream treat.

 Today Only! $1.00   How many dollars does she have left now?

$ __5__ .00 .

4. Alesha walks to the pet store to buy three new fish for her fish tank.

$1.00 each

How much money does Alesha have left after all her shopping?

$ __2__ .00 .

What Is Money?

Money is made of metal. Money is made of paper.
Circle the money made of metal. Put an **X** over the money made of paper.

People earn money by working.

When you buy something, you give away some of your money.
If the ice cream cone costs 75¢, what coins would you use to buy it?

__3__ quarters

Name _____

Circle the place where you will need money.

Money has value. Here are some of the coins we have in the United States.

1. Which coin is worth 25¢? penny nickel dime (quarter)

2. Which coin is worth 5¢? penny (nickel) dime quarter

3. Which coin is worth 1¢? (penny) nickel (dime) quarter

4. Which coin is worth 10¢? penny nickel (dime) quarter

5. Write the number of coins it would take to equal a quarter:

 = __2__ dimes + __1__ nickels.

OR = __5__ nickels

6. Write the number of coins it would take to equal a dime:

= __1__ nickels + __5__ pennies

OR = __10__ pennies

Name _____

Money on Parade!

Time for a parade! Write the answers in the blanks.

Look at the pennies! We count them by __1__ s.
Each penny in the band is worth __1__ ¢.

There go the nickels! We count them by __5__ s.
Each nickel clown is worth __5__ ¢.

Here are the dimes! We count them by __10__ s.
Each dime balloon is worth __10__ ¢.

Name _____

Here come the quarters! They are worth even more! Each quarter wheel is worth __25__ ¢.

Look at the dollars! They are paper, not coins. Each dollar flag is worth __100__ pennies!

Here is the money from the parade! Draw a line to match each piece of money with its value.

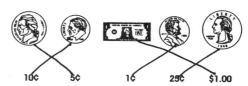

10¢ 5¢ 1¢ 25¢ $1.00

What was your favorite thing in the parade? _____
__Answers will vary.__
